MW00824325

CHRIST AT WORK
ORTHODOX CHRISTIAN
PERSPECTIVES ON VOCATION

CHRIST AT WORK

ORTHODOX CHRISTIAN PERSPECTIVES ON VOCATION

Edited
by
Ann Mitsakos Bezzerides

HOLY CROSS ORTHODOX PRESS
Brookline, Massachusetts

© Copyright 2006 Holy Cross Orthodox Press
Published by Holy Cross Orthodox Press
50 Goddard Avenue
Brookline, Massachusetts 02445

All rights reserved. No part of this publication may be reproduced, stored in a retrieval system, or transmitted in any form or by any means—electronic, mechanical, photocopy, recording, or any other—without the prior written permission of the publisher. The only exception is brief quotations in printed reviews.

ISBN 1-885652-87-9

On the cover: Detail of Ravenna mosaic; Peter and Andrew abandon fishing nets to follow Christ.

LIBRARY OF CONGRESS CATALOGING–IN–PUBLICATION DATA

Christ at work : Orthodox Christian perspectives on vocation / edited by Ann Mitsakos Bezzerides.
p.   cm.
ISBN 1-885652-87-9 (pbk. : alk. paper)
1. Vocation--Christianity. 2. Orthodox Eastern Church--Doctrines. I. Bezzerides, Ann Mitsakos.
BX323.C485 2006
248.4'819--dc22   2005037753

CONTENTS

Acknowledgments

This book is born out of a challenge. The challenge was by way of a grant to Hellenic College, a small Greek Orthodox college in Brookline, Massachusetts, from the Lilly Endowment Inc. for "the theological exploration of vocation." The challenge was that at Hellenic College, we now had to call to life programs addressing this theme, while asking ourselves the hard question, "What *is* the Orthodox Christian theological exploration of vocation?" Other Christian traditions could readily draw guidance from an array of theological writings on vocation to answer the question for their contexts. For the Orthodox, while there is much to be said and many indirect sources for vocation exploration (to which the authors of this collection bear witness), little recent work on vocation by Orthodox theologians was available for us to use as resource material.

The authors of this collection responded to my plea to offer wisdom on vocation from their areas of theological interest and scholarly study. With one exception, they hail from either St Vladimir's Orthodox Theological Seminary or from Hellenic College and Holy Cross Greek Orthodox School of Theology. It was my pleasure to include also a scholar from Weston Jesuit School of Theology who is of the Melkite Greek Catholic Church and is deeply immersed in the sources that Eastern Christian traditions draw upon for wisdom. I am deeply thankful for the time and effort of these theologians, for their work has already been used to enrich the programs and events of the grant-funded Office of Vocation and Ministry at Hellenic College. The conversation on Orthodox Christian vocation has begun, and we pray it will bear fruit.

This volume would not be possible without the intelligent foresight of people at Lilly Endowment Inc. who recognized the need for the theological exploration of vocation on college campuses. Their generosity and wisdom in steering the national initiative is remarkable. Thanks are also due to Hellenic College faculty, staff and students, and CrossRoad program staff, who were the first to hear and respond to the oral presentations of many of these papers, and have been vital conversation partners in this endeavor. Melanie DiStefano, Timothy Patitsas, Natasha Smith and Julia Wickes were careful readers of various papers, and offered extremely helpful feedback to the editor. Finally, much was needed by way of administrative support to make the seminar and this collection possible, and for this I am thoroughly grateful to Joshua Boyd, Melanie DiStefano, Stephanie Skedros and Natasha Smith.

Introduction

What should I do with my life? What should I major in? What career should I choose? Should I get married? What if I can't find a job that I want? How do I balance work and family life? Twenty-first century North Americans struggle with questions of vocation and calling, and parish priests, spiritual fathers, lay counselors, parents, teachers, youth workers – those whom we regularly turn to for guidance – affirm this.

Anxiety often accompanies this struggle with questions about vocation – whose advice to take, what resources to use, which experiences to trust. To what extent do I listen to the desires of my parents? Which types of career and personality tests will help me make an intelligent choice? Are any societal pressures valid? Should I change my job if I don't feel fulfilled? To what extent should income be a deciding factor in my career choices? Am I spending enough time with my family?

Careful discernment is necessary to answer these questions. For Orthodox Christians, the matrix of discernment is formed in prayer and fasting, repentance and confession, seeking wisdom from the rhythm of the liturgical year, and from a spiritual father. Living this tradition as "Scripture rightly interpreted"[1] enables us to have the Word of God continually in our mouths, circumcising our hearts and renewing our minds. Ultimately, this tradition enables us to hear and

1

see the wisdom of our Father in heaven through his Word, Jesus Christ, and his Holy Spirit.

This said, however, another barrage of questions ensues: Does God call us directly? If so, how? What if, in our seeking, we receive contradictory advice? These questions lead us to a prayerful, Christ-focused search to do "good theology." Our Church tradition illustrates that theological inquiry – actively probing the depth, richness, and challenge of what it means to live a life in Christ – is a source of wisdom in our struggle. We have much to learn from theologians committed to probing the depth of the Orthodox Christian faith.

In a way, it is novel for Orthodox Christian theologians to tackle the topic of vocation directly. The "doctrine of vocation" is most often explained as evolving out of the Protestant Reformation: Martin Luther is widely recognized as the first to challenge the standard paradigm of vocation as the division between the "religious life" followed by priests and monastics and the "ordinary life" of lay Christians.[2] John Calvin is also a key source for exploring the topic of vocation, as he includes theological reflections on "The Lord's calling as a basis of our way of life," and on "Outer and inner call" in his *Institutes of the Christian Religion* (1559).[3] Indeed, contemporary treatments of vocation include nothing of an Eastern Orthodox perspective, and recount the history of vocation with scarce mention of Eastern Christian texts and traditions. There is good reason for this: while there are Orthodox texts that speak to vocation, a reader is hard-pressed to find any direct, developed treatment of vocation as such, unless one includes texts on the priesthood, monasticism, and celibacy (but even these do not usually present themselves as specifically addressing 'vocation').[4]

What the authors represented in this volume reveal, however, is that Orthodox theologians have much to offer the conversation. We are grateful to friends at the Lilly Endowment Inc. who have recognized the active struggle with questions of vocation and calling in the United States today and who have made this publication possible. Through a generous grant from the Lilly Endowment Inc. to Hellenic College for "the theological exploration of vocation," the college was blessed to begin to work out this exploration in an Orthodox Christian context. Many of the authors of the articles in this volume visited the Hellenic College campus and spoke on the topic of vocation, sparking conversations that, among other things, have found their way into the program planning of the new Office of Vocation and Ministry.

Articles collected herein are meant for any Christian who wrestles with questions of vocation and desires to root his or her search within an orthodox faith in Christ. These texts will be especially useful to local chapters of Orthodox Christian Fellowship (OCF) groups on college campuses nationwide, which are able to apply for mini-grants to support their own "theological exploration of vocation." The texts are also part of the wider ecumenical conversation on vocation taking place among the eighty-eight religiously-affiliated colleges that have been granted similar funding.

Each of the theologians included in this book approaches the topic of vocation from his or her particular area of theological interest and scholarly study. The first three of the texts are authored by scholars of Scripture who use the Bible as their primary source. Too often, Orthodox Christians define themselves (and are defined by others) as entrenched in tradition, while Scripture takes a back seat. Recent Orthodox Christian theologians have reclaimed the primacy of the Scriptures, and this primacy is represented in these texts. The next two articles synthesize what church fathers – early patristic theologians to whom Eastern Christians continually turn for wisdom – have to offer as far as the theological exploration of vocation. The final three papers weave together a variety of sources to contribute three significant pieces to an Orthodox mosaic: the call of the Virgin Mary, vocation and ethics, and the priesthood of the laity. While there is much still to be written on Orthodoxy and vocation, this collection represents a useful beginning.

The article by Paul Nadim Tarazi, "Pursuing the Mind of Christ: Lessons on Vocation from the Old Testament," warns against an approach that simply cites New Testament texts related to individual talents and gifts and then concludes that the development and application of these gifts constitutes the fulfillment of one's Christian vocation. Rather, vocation exploration entails the Christian community seeking the "mind of Christ" (Phil 2:1-6). To seek the mind of Christ is to seek to know the true identity of Christ as conveyed throughout the whole of Scripture. Tarazi reviews the Old Testament to present the overall intention and unity of the text, so that we do not miss the most fundamental lessons about vocation: "We are called to assist our needy neighbor without regard to whether they are Christian or pagan, inside the Church or outside it, appealing or repulsive, acceptable or unacceptable in society." Tarazi's article, moreover, underscores the notion that vocational exploration must be integrated with a dogged attention to the scriptural story in its entirety.

John Barnet begins his article, "Seek First His Kingdom: An Invitation to Christian Vocation," with the provocative anecdote of his seeking vocation advice from the abbot of an Orthodox monastery. The abbot responded to his question of vocation by saying, "God doesn't care...God only cares that you seek first his kingdom." Barnet shows Christ's exhortation to "seek first the kingdom of God" to be strikingly pertinent to vocational exploration. Often our questions about vocation are born out of earthly anxiety and not compatible with discipleship. To be anxious is to have, essentially, a divided heart, one that is not pure and singular in its intention; discipleship entails, rather, seeking first God's kingdom, which is "to possess the understanding and intention of God himself." God ultimately reveals to us our one true vocation – to witness to the word of the kingdom of God – by transforming our hearts, the seat of our understanding and intention. Barnet concludes that the most important question is, then, not, "What shall I do?" but rather, "How shall I witness in whatever I do?" His article should be read in tandem with the Gospel of St. Matthew.

The wisdom of the abbot in Barnet's article is remarkably similar to that of an elder referred to in Theodore Stylianopoulos' article, "'A Life Worthy of God': Vocation according to St. Paul." Stylianopoulos tells the anecdote of a young seminary student consulting a beloved bishop about his future. The bishop replied, "Do whatever you like, whatever comes your way, but do it well as a Christian. Whatever you choose, do it for the love of God and the service of others." Stylianopoulos explores vocation according to St. Paul through three fundamental questions – who to be, what to be, and how to be. St. Paul's answers to these questions are "as-

tonishingly God-centered and community-centered
in ways that many might find difficult to conceive in
modern times." While St. Paul's exceedingly dramatic
experience on the road to Damascus was unique, this
did not preclude the Apostle's view that all Christians
have a special calling – the universal message of salvation to share equally in the blessings of God's new
revelation in Christ. St. Paul does not address directly
how a Christian is to know his or her particular calling, but rather "takes for granted that the Holy Spirit,
palpably acting in the life of the Church, motivated
and led Christians to express their particular gifts and
fulfill their specific calling guided by love." No role
within the body of Christ was considered secondary or
useless; all contributed to the upbuilding of the community. Stylianopoulos presents a rich lesson on the
fundamental questions of life, rooted in the teachings
of St. Paul.

Khaled Anatolios, in "Considering Vocation: The
Witness of the Fathers," offers a patristic response to
the dilemma of identifying one's vocation in contemporary Western society. He argues that there is no objective standard of truth or morality in today's culture,
and therefore no coherent "world" wherein the human
self can find a natural home. Conversely, the Fathers
of the Church believed in objective standards of value,
and the necessity of living one's life accordingly: God
has ordained human beings to live in a certain way
(purely), and with a certain goal (union with Christ).
"Vocation" – whose etymological root implies a calling
– becomes problematic when it does not entail an "other" to do the calling. In his exploration, Anatolios em-
ploys the threefold path of purification, illumination,
and divinization preferred by, among other Fathers,

St. Maximos the Confessor. He shows how the human search for vocation must be cleansed, educated, and deified. Both subjectively, in terms of the desires we bring to the search for calling, and objectively, in terms of the cosmic fittingness of work we might do, this threefold structure perfects the human search for calling by helping to see the truth about the self, the world, and God.

In the mystical theology developed by early Christian theologians, Demetrios Katos finds clear lessons for how secular vocations can be made sacred. Mystical theology contributes a vision of what we *are* and what we might *become* through speaking of reality from a divine perspective. We are all called to become a divine image of our Creator, and this call means that all human activity can be sanctified. In his article, "In the Image of God: Mystical Theology and Secular Vocations," Katos asserts, "We do not become spiritual by abandoning human activity, but by transforming it." The vocational search is not a problem to be confronted, but an opportunity to grow and mature, motivated by the potential revealed to us in Jesus Christ. The self, the body, society, and one's work within it can all be captured for Christ, provided we manage to recognize our goal in God, and then freely choose the difficult course that will make that union a reality. Katos draws on the rich wisdom of the Fathers to show how integral this vision was to early church theologians. Reflecting God's glory by living the freedom entrusted to us in Christ and loving our fellow humans, in whatever setting, fulfills our ultimate calling.

Deborah Malacky Belonick uses both scriptural passages and meditations of Christian theologians throughout the centuries to reflect upon the life of the Virgin Mary as related to hearing and answering God's call in her article, "The Call of the Virgin Mary." The integrity and character of the Mother of God, her response to God's bidding, and her personal struggle to fulfill God's purpose provide all believers with lessons in discernment regarding their own vocations. The Theotokos' life represents the pinnacle of human vocation because, struggling to the end with her own calling, she became, as Orthodox hymnology commonly reminds the believer, "more honorable than the cherubim and more glorious beyond compare than the seraphim." Emphasizing both the personal and the communal nature of the life in Christ, Belonick invites readers to walk to the path of the Virgin Mary and to cry with her, "My spirit rejoices in God my Savior" (Luke 1:47).

Stanley Harakas, in "Vocation and Ethics," provides a good background for the response of a bishop or abbot to the question of vocation, "God doesn't care." Harakas argues that God is not "a celestial employment agency." He challenges the notion that "anyone who is a wife or husband, an employer, an employee, a factory worker, a salesperson, and so on, precisely and exclusively because of that status or role, has a specific calling from God to be that and not something else." He argues that the New Testament and patristic tradition have only one definition for "calling" and that is the calling of persons to follow Christ for salvation. Too often "calling" or "vocation" has become another secular term for what we determine are our desires. He advocates for an important distinction: it is *the way in which* an Orthodox Christian approaches these roles and occupations that is of the essence. Because this calling must always be incarnated in real experience, calling and vocation are by definition integrally and ethically related. Vocation deals with values, choices, decisions, and commitments. Ethical requirements are central to any calling or vocation, whether to the priesthood, the celibate, monastic, or married life, or to the calling to use one's inherent, God-given gifts for the upbuilding of the Church and enriching of the common good. Moreover, Harakas emphasizes that integrity is foundational in the ethical dimension of vocation within the Christian life.

Finally, Paul Meyendorff redeems the notion of "The Priesthood of the Laity" for Orthodox Christians. He acknowledges that Orthodox Christians have largely forgotten the notion that the laity comprise a royal priesthood; instead, "priesthood" immediately is connected with ordained clergy, bishops and priests. Meyendorff reminds us that in the New Testament, the term priest is used either for Christ, the one "high priest," or for all the faithful baptized, but never for ordained Christian clergy; only in later centuries was the notion of priesthood attached to ordained ministry. His article examines the meaning of priesthood as expressed in the Epistle to the Hebrews and in the liturgy. He concludes from Scripture and liturgy that every Christian is a priest, called to bring God's divine love and forgiveness to the world. He purports that the function of the ordained clergy in the Orthodox Church is to maintain and promote order within the church and to enable all the baptized to exercise their own priestly ministry of Christ, received in the baptismal font. He also explains that ordained clergy will usually carry out their mission within the local church community, while baptized Christians are called to exercise their priestly vocation in the world.

The definition of "vocation" was not given or determined before we asked the scholars to write. To read
their papers is to discern certain distinctions in the way
the term is defined and used. Readers may determine
and debate these potential distinctions; I am struck
more by the commonalities. In fact, through the repetition of significant themes throughout the papers, we
were able to devise a theological definition of vocation
that encompasses the wisdom of these authors and
forms a starting point for the Orthodox Christian theological exploration of vocation: *Vocation is one's ongoing
and unique way of being in the world that is a response to
Christ's call to love God with heart, soul, mind, and strength,
and one's neighbor as oneself.*

With this "definition," we locate vocation as our *response* to God's initiative in first creating and loving us,
and in offering his only begotten Son for the salvation
of our souls. The lives of sincere Orthodox Christians
will reflect ongoing gratitude for this offer of salvation – a response of love that engages the entire being:
heart, soul, mind and strength. As such, no two people
will respond in identical ways. Finally, and most im-
portantly, the definition acknowledges that God-given
vocation is borne out in community because it is a response to the call to love the neighbor. Vocation must
entail discovering how each of us will uniquely love
our neighbor: both the neighbor within the same socio-
economic or faith group, and also the neighbor that is
not of the same "tribe," ethnic group, socio-economic
class, or geographic region – especially the neighbor
in need. True vocation is a life lived for God and the
neighbor – it is, in the words of Stylianopoulos, "astonishingly God-centered and community-centered."

The ongoing process of discovering this unique response requires careful, ongoing discernment that may be guided well by the Orthodox cycle of feasts and fasts, and prayer, repentance, confession and Communion, all of which invite us to a rich life in Christ. Discerning how to use God-given gifts to best serve him and love the neighbor, given the practical circumstances of life, is an incredible challenge – a great, holy challenge. When we live life as vocation, we witness to the word of the kingdom of God and rejoice in that gift that gives ultimate meaning to our daily, complex lives. May this volume orient our thinking to the beauty of this process and lead us to fruitful purpose: transformation today and eternal life in Christ tomorrow.

Ann Mitsakos Bezzerides
Annunciation 2005

Works Cited in Introduction

Alexandra, Mother. "The Monastic Vocation in America." In *Orthodox Perspectives on Pastoral Praxis*, 185-87. Brookline, MA: Holy Cross Orthodox Press, 1988.

Badcock, Gary D. *The Way of Life : A Theology of Christian Vocation*. Grand Rapids MI: W.B. Eerdmans Publishing, 1998.

Behr, John. *The Way to Nicea*. Vol. 1, *The Formation of Christian Theology*. Crestwood, NY: St Vladimir's Seminary Press, 2001.

Cartwright, Michael G. "Theological Exploration of Vocations: Recommended Readings/an Annotated List of Protestant Reflections." Lantz Center for Christian Vocations, 2001.

Hopko, Thomas. "An Orthodox Statement." In *To Be a Priest: Perspectives on Vocation and Ordination*, edited by Urban T. Holmes. New York: Seabury Press, 1975.

Notes

1 For a full development of this notion for Orthodox Christians, see John Behr, *The Way to Nicea*, vol. 1, *The Formation of Christian Theology* (Crestwood, NY: St. Vladimir's Seminary Press, 2001).

2 See Gary D. Badcock, *The Way of Life: A Theology of Christian Vocation* (Grand Rapids, MI: W.B. Eerdmans Publishing, 1998), ch. 3; Michael G. Cartwright, "Theological Exploration of Vocations: Recommended Readings/an Annotated List of Protestant Reflections" (Lantz Center for Christian Vocations, 2001), 1.

3 Cartwright, "Theological Exploration of Vocations: Recommended Readings/an Annotated List of Protestant Reflections," 1.

4 A noteworthy exception of an Orthodox Christian pastoral approach to vocation is a short article, "Finding One's Calling in Life," by Thomas Hopko, published in an Orthodox Education Day booklet at St. Vladimir's Orthodox Theological Seminary, 1997, and accessible at http://www.svots.edu/Events/Orthodox-Education-Day/Articles/1996-Fr-Thomas-Hopko.html. Two short articles that deal with the priesthood and monasticism as vocation are: Mother Alexandra, "The Monastic Vocation in America," in *Orthodox Perspectives on Pastoral Praxis* (Brookline, MA: Holy Cross Orthodox Press, 1988), Thomas Hopko, "An Orthodox Statement," in *To Be a Priest: Perspectives on Vocation and Ordination*, ed. Urban T. Holmes (New York: Seabury Press, 1975).

Pursuing the Mind of Christ: Lessons on Vocation from the Old Testament

PAUL NADIM TARAZI

Introduction

Why should Christians search the Old Testament for lessons on Christian vocation? The New Testament seems to address the issue adequately. For example, Matthew 24:14-30 tells the famous "parable of the talents." Servants are entrusted with a portion of their master's property; when they later return the investment with or without interest, they are rewarded or punished according to their efforts. This simple analogy may be used for our role as Orthodox Christians today: God has given each of us "talents" and we must use them wisely to gain an eternal reward. Other places in the New Testament underscore this view. St. Paul writes in Romans 12:6, "Having gifts (*charismata*) that differ according to the grace given to us, let us use them." St. Peter writes in 1 Peter 4:10, "As each has received a gift, employ it for one another, as good stewards of God's varied grace." Every Christian, then, is given a personal gift or talents, and the obligation to use them to God's glory. How may each person's gift be discerned? It seems natural to understand one's innate talents as given by God, and therefore their devel-

13

opment and application in life as fulfillment of one's
Christian vocation.

Perhaps, however, the matter is not so simple. St.
Paul also writes that we are to take Christ himself as
our example in conducting our lives before God. In
Philippians 2:1-6, in a passage in which St. Paul is exhorting the Philippians to unity, he enjoins his readers
to imitate the humility of Christ in all their dealings:

> ... complete my joy by being of the same *mind*, having
> the same love, being in full accord and of one *mind*. Do
> nothing from selfishness or conceit, but in humility
> count others better than yourselves. Let each of you
> look not only to his own interests, but also to the
> interests of others. Have this *mind* among yourselves,
> which is yours in Christ Jesus, who, though he was in
> the form of God, did not count equality with God a
> thing to be grasped, but humbled himself... (emphasis
> added)

To notice the emphasis in this passage on "mind" is
to realize that for Paul, if a community is to be of one
mind, united in the same love, this community must
have the mind of Christ. This "mind of Christ" – best
defined as a set of principles and understandings con-
sonant with the humility and compassion of Christ –
immediately requires a context from which these principles and understanding can be acquired, and that can
be authoritatively said to be "of Christ." And because
the "common mind" of believers must necessarily be
one that can be communicated and taught, its nature
must necessarily be linguistic.[1]

Already we are within reach of the introduction to
the Gospel of John, in which Christ is explicitly identified with the divine Word (Greek *logos*), which not
only "was with God" but also "was God" (John 1:1).[2]

Certainly the New Testament writers did not fashion their message from thin air. Rather, they sought to clothe their claims of Jesus' divinity and messiahship in the scriptural fabric of the only divine Word they and their contemporary audiences acknowledged, their Bible: the Old Testament. Here, then, is the proper context for acquiring "the mind of Christ" (1 Cor 2:16). To seek to model one's life on Christ, the Word of God, requires that one understand not only the New Testament but also the Old Testament, equally the Word (Hebrew *dabar*, the equivalent of *logos*) of God.

Paul's exhortation to have the mind of Christ was not only directed at the leaders of the Philippian community – "the bishops and deacons" – but "to all the saints in Christ Jesus who are at Philippi" (Phil 1:1). If we, today, join with the Philippian community as addressees of Paul's gospel, then our first vocation is to have the mind of Christ. To make sure that it is truly *Christ's mind* that we are striving for, we must continually seek this Christ of the New Testament, whose identity is woven from the fabric of the Word of the Old Testament. If we do not know this Word, we risk gravely misunderstanding who Christ is. Our first vocation is, therefore, to continually seek to know and be formed by this Word.

Much of modern scholarship of the Bible has fractured it into thousands of irreconcilable parts; our Christian calling, in line with the Orthodox exegetical tradition, is to see these Scriptures as indeed a unified whole, as truly the Word of God: "Paul, a servant of Jesus Christ, called to be an apostle, set apart for the gospel of God which he promised beforehand through his prophets in the holy Scriptures, the gospel concerning his Son" (Rom 1:1-3a); "Think not that I have come to abolish the law and the prophets; I have come not to abolish them but to fulfill them. For truly, I say to you, till heaven and earth pass away, not an iota, not a dot, will pass from the law until all is accomplished" (Matt 5:17-18). St. John Chrysostom is a prominent early Church father who took so seriously this unity of the Bible that throughout his verse-by-verse homiletical commentaries on numerous scriptural books, he easily cites or alludes to other books of the bible to support or illustrate his interpretation. In commenting on Isaiah 1:11 he says, "The whole of Psalm 49 dwells on this point, though it uses different words to weave the same ideas. What we have in the psalm…is equivalent."[3] This method was part of an important understanding regarding scriptural interpretation: "We are not the lords over the rules of interpretation, but must pursue Scripture's interpretation of itself."[4] It is by following this line of thought that I proceed here, so that a full understanding of the Old Testament may function as foundational to the formation of "the mind of Christ."[5]

The Old Testament is commonly categorized into three main literary divisions (or "scriptures") – divisions that must be understood as essential building blocks for this mind of Christ. The Law[6] tells the story of God's creation and ordering of the world, his selection of a chosen people, and his interactions with his people until they are poised to enter their promised homeland. The Prophets[7] tell the story of his people's entrance into and then exile from their homeland, and finally of his people's access to the new heavenly Jerusalem, their real homeland. The third division, Psalms and Wisdom literature,[8] is a collection of piety, advice, and philosophical reflection. At first glance, this third division seems out of place in this narrative structure. Further examination reveals, however, Wisdom's absolutely crucial role within the Old Testament and by extension for the New Testament, and therefore a unified scriptural understanding of vocation.

The Torah: God's Law of Instruction

This first part of the Bible comprises its first five books, as can be deduced from their collective name in Greek, the Pentateuch. In Hebrew, however, this section is named the Torah (*torah*). While usually translated as "law," *torah* more properly connotes "instruction," specifically divine instruction which includes an element of command.[9] This sets out the clear pattern that Scripture operates within the verbal realm. God's definitive approach to his people is through his word of instruction and command, his *torah*.

God's *torah* is addressed specifically to Israel, but by extension to all mankind. The biblical story of a relationship between God and man begins not when God promises to make of Abram "a great nation" (Gen 12:2), but with the creation of mankind as a whole, represented in the figures of Adam ("man," Gen 1:26) and Eve ("life," Gen 3:20). After God decides to wipe his creation clean because of the unwelcome spread of sin throughout the human realm, he makes his first covenant with Noah in Genesis 6:18 and 9:9-11, guaranteeing the continuation of human life through his promise "that never again shall *all flesh* be cut off by the waters of a flood, and never again shall there be a flood to destroy the earth" (emphasis added). Even God's promise to Abram to make him the father of a great nation extends the benefit to the entire creation: "By you all families of the earth shall bless themselves." God's actual covenant with Abram in Genesis 17:1-14 further specifies its universal implications:

> Behold, my covenant is with you, and you shall be the father of a multitude of nations ... I will make you exceedingly fruitful; and I will make nations of you, and kings shall come forth from you. And I will establish my covenant between me and you and your descendants after you throughout their generations for an everlasting covenant, to be God to you and to your descendants after you.

The word "covenant" (Heb. *b*e*rit*, or "agreement") is itself a formal term that connotes "binding obligation," and is therefore not only a blessing to Abraham but also an instruction, *torah*. Abraham's descendents do not benefit from the covenant through attaining status over other peoples. Indeed, Ezekiel warns Israel that they are of the same stuff as the other nations – "Your origin and your birth are of the land of the Canaanites; your father was an Amorite, and your mother a Hittite" (Ezek 16:3, 45) – and so inextricably linked to them. Abraham buries his wife – the mother of the new people of God, no less – not on his own hereditary land or land promised by God, but on land he has to purchase from a Hittite, one of "the people of the land" (Gen 23). God's renaming of Abram (Heb "exalted father") to Abraham (Heb "father of a multitude") in Genesis 17:5 is itself a sign that God's purpose for his people is outward rather than inward, universal rather than local.

Here we approach the very heart of God's torachic intent. Just before the people enter the promised land, Moses renews God's covenant with them by reciting the *torah* to them, beginning with the Great

Commandment: "The Lord our God is one Lord; and you shall love the Lord your God with all your heart, and with all your soul, and with all your might" (Deut 6:4-5). The same Hebrew word *'ahab* that describes the love to be offered to God is used in Leviticus 19 (part of that book's famous "Holiness Code") to refer to the love that must be offered to one's neighbor (Lev 19:18), and even to "the stranger who sojourns with you [who must be treated as a] native among you, and you shall love him as yourself; for you were strangers in the land of Egypt" (Lev 19:34). God instructs his people to understand their collective identity as a gift from him, and to demonstrate that awareness always by looking outside themselves to the vulnerable neighbor, to the stranger, the one who *needs* love.

The benefit, then, brought by the covenant with Abraham's descendants is that they are blessed with the obligation to carry the *torah* of God to the other nations. In the covenant with Abraham, the reader is reminded, "He that is eight days old among you shall be circumcised; every male throughout your generations, whether born in your house, or bought with your money from any foreigner who is not of your offspring, both he that is born in your house and he that is bought with your money, shall be circumcised." (Gen 17:12-13). However, membership in the covenant does not grant authority over the divine instruction, but the reverse: Israel is itself kept (that is, protected) by the *torah* inasmuch as Israel keeps (that is, observes and applies) the *torah*.

To this effect, God's instruction pervades the Torah. Moses' introduction to his reading of the law in Deuteronomy is the best example:

Now this is the commandment, the statutes and the ordinances which the Lord your God commanded me to teach you, that you may do them in the land to which you are going over, to possess it; that you may fear the Lord your God, you and your son and your son's son, by keeping all his statutes and his commandments, which I command you, all the days of your life; and that your days may be prolonged. Hear therefore, O Israel, and be careful to do them; that it may go well with you, and that you may multiply greatly, as the Lord, the God of your fathers, has promised you, in a land flowing with milk and honey. (Deut 6:1-3)

The practice among Hasidic rabbis of clutching the scroll of the law to themselves as they bring it into their synagogues, as if it were a life preserver, demonstrates this principle liturgically. So does the Eastern Christian singing of the hymn "Come, let us bow down to Christ" while the book of the Gospels is brought by the priest into the church's sanctuary. The scroll rests in the place of honor in the synagogue, just as the book of the Gospels does in the church. Christians as well as Jews face the questions: Do we keep this book, or does this book keep us? Does the book belong to us, or we to the book? If forsaking the book, the Word of God, means that we will be forsaken by God, then Paul's assertion, "whatever the law says it speaks to those who are under the law, so that every mouth may be stopped, and the whole world may be held accountable to God" (Rom 3:19) implies that the book is the expression of the presence of God with us, and in fact functions *as* the mind and will of God for us.

In the ancient world, the believer had two ways to approach the divine: through its statue, by going to the deity's temple and viewing the statue, or through listening to that deity's oracles, utterances, and teachings. However, the divine statues and their temples proved to be costly and thus a burden on the worshipers. Furthermore, the statues were after all images from the created domain to the effect that one would be worshiping creatures as deities.[10] This idolatry, or creation of a god in one's own image or images from our world, challenges God's absolute authority and initiative, which is why, on the one hand, the Old Testament stringently and absolutely condemns images of the divine,[11] while on the other hand, it speaks ironically of the divine statues.[12] Consequently, Scripture leaves believers in the biblical God with only God's words – his instruction, his *torah* – as the legitimate way to know him and his will. Thus, in the Torah, after sin sends God's creation awry, God's new covenant with his people happens specifically and exclusively through man's acquisition of a new perspective from God's verbal instruction. And this instruction of the Torah demands that believers make it their *vocation* to look outside their own individual and community concerns and address the needs of the vulnerable neighbor, the stranger, the disadvantaged man or woman without help or friends.

The Prophets: Speakers of God's Word

If the first part of the Old Testament recounts the story of God and man from creation up to the point where Israel is poised to enter the promised land of Canaan, then the second part, the Prophets (*nebi'im*), continues the story from the people's entrance into the land to the point at which they are forcibly led out of the land again by foreign conquerors, and finally to their eventual return. And just as the utterances of God (rather than the image of God) determine the course of the story in the Torah, so in the Prophets the divine word (*debar yahweh*) inexorably dictates and conditions the story's continuation. The story is told directly in the first part of the Prophets, the Former Prophets (the books of Joshua through 2 Kings) and indirectly in its second part, the Latter Prophets (the books of Isaiah, Jeremiah, Ezekiel, and the Scroll of the Twelve Prophets).

The Former Prophets begin with the entrance of the people of Israel into the promised land; the people first conquer and then settle the land under the leadership of Joshua (Hebrew *yehoshua'*, "the Lord saves"). Through this, God is seen as upholding his people, fulfilling a crucial part of his covenant with Israel – the covenant first expressed to Abraham (Gen 12:7) and then to Moses (Exod 3:8). The people have found salvation in the terms laid out by the covenant: blessing and stability from God in a land of their own, as long as they are faithful hearers and doers of God's *torah*: "And Israel served the Lord all the days of Joshua, and all the days of the elders who outlived Joshua and had known all the work which the Lord did for Israel" (Josh 24:31; Judg 2:7). But this peaceful situation unravels almost immediately. The generation that follows Joshua's does not "know the Lord or the work which he had done for Israel" (Judg 2:10); their apostasy in favor of other gods provokes God first to anger, then to punishing them for breaking the covenant.

Thereafter, the story follows the same cyclic pattern. The people of Israel sin against God by breaking the terms of the covenant; God punishes them; the people repent of their sin; and God mercifully restores them to favor. God expresses his will not through official representatives of the people, but through his own representatives, the prophets, who serve neither temples nor rulers but the *Debar Yahweh* which God commands them to utter (often against their own desire to avoid notoriety).[13] Against the people's desire to serve themselves rather than their neighbor, and to follow the more predictable, user-friendly gods of neighboring societies, the prophets continually pit God's demand to follow the terms of the covenant, remain faithful to him, and care for the vulnerable, the weak, and the outsider. Nowhere in the Bible is the prophetic message expressed more forcefully and vividly than in Jeremiah 7:1-10:

> The word that came to Jeremiah from the Lord: "Stand in the gate of the Lord's house, and proclaim there this word, and say, Hear the word of the Lord, all you men of Judah who enter these gates to worship the Lord. Thus says the Lord of hosts, the God of Israel, Amend your ways and your doings, and I will let you dwell in this place. Do not trust in these deceptive words: 'This is the temple of the Lord, the temple of the Lord, the temple of the Lord.' For if you truly amend your ways and your doings, if you truly execute justice one with another, if you do not oppress the alien, the fatherless or the widow, or shed innocent blood in this place, and if you do not go after other gods to your own hurt, then I will let you dwell in this place, in the land that I gave of old to your fathers for ever. Behold, you trust in deceptive words to no avail. Will you steal, murder, commit adultery, swear falsely, burn incense to Baal, and go after other gods that you have not known, and then come and stand before me in this house, which is called by my name, and say, 'We are delivered!' – only to go on doing all these abominations? Has this house, which is called by my name, become a den of robbers in your eyes? Behold, I myself have seen it, says the Lord.

The word of the Lord through Jeremiah is powerful indeed, stark in illuminating the contrast between the people's pursuits and what they are called to by God.

In the midst of this, the people yearn for a king, and this desire for kingly leadership is interpreted by the prophet Samuel as a further departure from trusting absolutely in God and his governing word (1 Sam 8:4-22). The first king, Saul, is a miserable failure, and neither David nor Solomon, the first kings God favors, escapes prophetic judgment. Nathan, the prophet who announces to David that God will make a covenant with him to establish his royal line forever (2 Sam 7:5-16), soon afterwards announces the Lord's punishment of David and his line (2 Sam 12:1-14) for David's adulterous liaison with Bathsheba and arranged murder of Uriah the Hittite, her husband and an outsider. Solomon, under whom all the tribes are briefly united and with whom God renews the earlier covenant with David (1 Kgs 9:1-5), nonetheless breaks faith with God by following the gods of his foreign wives, earning God's renewed condemnation and the reduction of the Davidic domain to the territory of the tribe of Judah (1 Kgs 11:1-13). With the exceptions of a few faithful kings such as Azariah and Jotham, and even with the brief revivals of observance of the Law under Hezekiah and Josiah, the descendents of Solomon (in the southern kingdom) and those of the upstart Jeroboam (in the northern kingdom) repeatedly "[do] what [is] evil in the sight of the Lord" (1 Kgs 14:22). This refrain, scandalous at first but through repetition becoming familiar and at last tedious, occurs no less than thirty-one times in 1 and 2 Kings. It underscores both kingdoms' abandonment of the Torah to such a profound degree that God subjects them to conquest and exile at the hands of foreign empires.

The grinding paradox implicit in these events (what God, after all, would allow his people's cities to be destroyed and the people led into exile?) is undermined by the reader's eventual desire to side with God on the matter. Israel's story follows the same repetitious pattern but never gets anywhere. The God who led Abraham *out of* the land of the Chaldeans has led Abraham's descendants *back into* that land's later manifestation, Babylonia, and is justified in doing so. The situation of salvation described in the book of Joshua (whose name, like those of the prophets Hosea and Isaiah, and Jesus as well, contains the Hebrew root for "salvation") has regressed ignominiously into a situation of renewed slavery. The only "success story" in the Latter Prophets is that of the divine word, expressed again and again by the prophets who were chosen by God to speak words of warning, condemnation, and promise on his behalf. The people abandon the covenant and devolve into abject turpitude; yet at the same time, the divine word grows and flowers in their midst, unflinchingly defining their sin for what it is, but also holding out hope of renewal and restoration in the eyes of God.

The Latter Prophets, with their twofold message of God's judgment and mercy, treat in depth the period between the establishment of the northern and southern kingdoms and the eve of the people's return from exile. The outer two books – Isaiah and the Scroll of the Twelve Prophets – address the overarching story of the fall and exile of Israel and Judah, whereas the inner two books – Jeremiah and Ezekiel – concentrate on the sin itself and the exile.[14] A fierce invective against Israel's and Judah's sinful unfaithfulness to the *torah* surrounds God's promise of mercy and redemption, that he will visit the people he exiled in order to call them into his new Jerusalem.

In Isaiah, the first of the outer two books, God's promise of comfort illustrates the close relationship between the essential story given in the Torah and the promise of return from exile: it is the only place in the Old Testament outside the book of Genesis where Sarah (the barren wife blessed by God to bring his people into being) is mentioned as well as Abraham.

> Hearken to me, you who pursue deliverance, you who seek the Lord; look to the rock from which you were hewn, and to the quarry from which you were dug. Look to Abraham your father and to Sarah who bore you; for when he was but one I called him, and I blessed him and made him many. For the Lord will comfort Zion; he will comfort all her waste places, and will make her wilderness like Eden, her desert like the garden of the Lord; joy and gladness will be found in her, thanksgiving and the voice of song. (Isa 51:1-3)

The next two verses bring out the paramount role played by God's word of instruction in the new divine economy, which (true to its nature, as illustrated above in the discussion of the Torah) looks outward to all of mankind:

> Listen to me, my people, and give ear to me, my nation; for a law will go forth from me, and my justice for a light to the peoples. My deliverance draws near speedily, my salvation has gone forth, and my arms will rule the peoples; the coastlands wait for me, and for my arm they hope.

The story in Isaiah has a strikingly similar pattern to the story in the Torah. Ultimately, in Isaiah the people are called as Abraham has been called in the Torah, to come out of their land of punishment and accept the authority of God through his word of instruction. The same pattern fits exactly the story of the exodus from Egypt and, before that, the story of Joseph's brothers. To these brothers, God shows mercy once they repent their sale of their brother into slavery, which in Leviticus 25:39 is condemned as a grave sin against the God who frees his people from slavery. What occurs in the Prophets occurs also in the Torah: one sins, one repents, one is saved by God through his mercy to once again observe his instruction. God's word saves; falling away from God's word brings destruction; God's mercy leads the penitent back to God's saving word.

The central books in the Latter Prophets, Jeremiah and Ezekiel, describe God's new covenant with the exiles – a covenant which is not wholly new. It restores the people to a state of acceptance and obedience towards God's word, but in a way yet unheard of. Ezekiel 11:17-20 makes the link between the new covenant and the heart of the people:

> Therefore say, "Thus says the Lord God: 'I will gather you from the peoples, and assemble you out of the countries where you have been scattered, and I will give you the land of Israel. And when they come there, they will remove from it all its detestable things and all its abominations. And I will give them one heart, and put a new spirit within them; I will take the stony heart out of their flesh and give them a heart of flesh, that they may walk in my statutes and keep my ordinances and obey them; and they shall be my people, and I will be their God.'"

Jeremiah 31:31-34 makes the point even more explicit:

> Behold, the days are coming, says the Lord, when I will make a new covenant with the house of Israel

and the house of Judah, not like the covenant which I made with their fathers when I took them by the hand to bring them out of the land of Egypt, my covenant which they broke, though I was their husband, says the Lord. But this is the covenant which I will make with the house of Israel after those days, says the Lord: I will put my law within them, and I will write it upon their hearts; and I will be their God, and they shall be my people. And no longer shall each man teach his neighbor and each his brother, saying, Know the Lord, for they shall all know me, from the least of them to the greatest, says the Lord; for I will forgive their iniquity, and I will remember their sin no more.

The same Jeremiah speaks often of this new beginning as a "return, turning (around)" (Hebrew *shub*) to indicate a turning of the heart, repentance (Jer 25:5; 26:3; 35:15; 36:3, 7). The same verb is employed to describe the people's return from exile in Babylon.[15] Thus, God promises that if the people will return to him, he will return to them. His prophetic and torachic word will not let them down or be without its intended effect: "For as the rain and the snow come down from heaven, and return not thither but water the earth, making it bring forth and sprout, giving seed to the sower and bread to the eater, so shall my word be that goes forth from my mouth; it shall not return to me empty, but it shall accomplish that which I purpose, and prosper in the thing for which I sent it" (Isa 55:10-11). The new Jerusalem, therefore, describes not so much a physical location as it does the honoring and keeping of the Torah by the believer who has turned back to God. Once all the barriers the people have erected between themselves and God have been swept away, they can return to him, and he to them, whether in Jerusalem, Babylon, or elsewhere.

But the Prophets do not tell a story with a happy ending, only a conditional one. Malachi, the last book in the Scroll of the Twelve Prophets, ends with a warning to remind the people that what has gone before can happen again: "Remember the law of my servant Moses, the statutes and ordinances that I commanded him at Horeb for all Israel. Behold, I will send you Elijah the prophet before the great and terrible day of the Lord comes. And he will turn the hearts of fathers to their children and the hearts of children to their fathers, lest I come and smite the land with a curse" (Mal 4:4-6). Suddenly, the reader is returned to the wilderness in Deuteronomy, deprived of any security he imagines he has outside God's call to his people to depend only on his word, which alone can save them.

In the prophetic books, it is made clear that kingship faltered, the city was destroyed and the people exiled because they did not take care of "the alien, the fatherless or the widow" and went "after other gods to [their] own hurt" (Jer 7:6). It is also made clear that the hope after the people's return from exile is the new city – the heavenly Jerusalem – where God himself will shepherd his people through his elect (Ezek 34 and 37:16ff.). What does this mean for us today? Being this new people of God, we must continually respond to God's calling in order to remain citizens, to be found worthy of the heavenly Jerusalem at our judgment. As we are members of the new David, Jesus Christ, we have to act the way he does, having his mind as our own.

The Writings: An Invitation to Know God's *TORAH*

It is easy to assume that the Torah and Prophets of-

fer the complete solution to the problem of Adam's fall
into sin. Both divine word and divine instruction define God's will as serving one's neighbor rather than
oneself. Cannot the conclusion be drawn that here, indeed, is found the basis of St. Paul's "mind... which is
yours in Christ Jesus" (Phil 2:5)? Is this not the context
from which Christians may derive their understanding
of Christian vocation? The answer is both yes and no.
Yes, because the Law and Prophets are nothing other
than the *debar yahweh* out of which the New Testament
writers constructed their portrait of Jesus the Word.
The answer is also no, however, because even taken
together, the Torah and Prophets are addressed solely
to Israel, the "chosen people," and concern Israel's affairs exclusively. Despite their insistence on loving the
neighbor and stranger, they can still be seen as a rule
book, a "mission statement," to be observed and kept
by the inside group but not by outsiders. Such exclusiv-
ity can only warp God's intent that Israel not only hear
and possess his *dabar*, but also carry it outside customary human boundaries – ethnic and religious as well
as political – to its neighbors. The Law and Prophets
contain God's solution to the problem of Adam's fall,
but they do not actually preach that message to their
intended outside audience. This incompleteness is addressed precisely by the Writings, which bring to the
Old Testament – and by extension to the question of
Christian vocation – the essential impulse needed to
make universal the message of the universal God.

Wisdom (*hokmah*) was a topic of universal interest
in the world created by Alexander of Macedon and
thus proved to be a workable channel for the authors
of the Writings to communicate their message to the
"nations," i.e., the world at large. In earlier tribal so-

cieties, wisdom was the domain of the tribe's council of elders. It was, therefore, a communal affair and figured highly in the decisions of the tribe's patriarch. In a holdover from tribal society, a nation's king was also regarded as the "father" of his people, the source of divine judgment (Hebrew *mishpat*) among them. Because the king could not always preside over every dispute, he also wielded the law, the written codification of oral traditions of justice. Royal wisdom and the law were both viewed as gifts from the deity to the king upon his ascension to the throne: the law as the set of guidelines according to which *mishpat* could be correctly dispensed, and *hokmah* as the personal quality of understanding and knowledge that ensured that the law would be put to its intended purpose. To understand how crucial wisdom's role was in ancient Near Eastern society, one has only to recall the stories in 1 Kings and 2 Chronicles of Solomon's wisdom, which was so renowned throughout the world, according to the biblical author, that even a foreign ruler, the Queen of Sheba, sought his counsel (1 Kgs 10:1-13).

But wisdom was not exclusively a matter of religion or royalty. It was as directly available to the least commoner as to the king:

> Wisdom cries aloud in the street; in the markets she raises her voice; on the top of the walls she cries out; at the entrance of the city gates she speaks: "How long, O simple ones, will you love being simple? How long will scoffers delight in their scoffing and fools hate knowledge? Give heed to my reproof; behold, I will pour out my thoughts to you; I will make my words known to you. (Prov 1:20-23)

This passage reflects ancient Near Eastern social convention in that it locates wisdom's realm at the city gates. An ancient Near Eastern nation comprised a city and its surrounding lands, and the true meeting-places for different nations and cultures were where insider and outsider met regularly. Here, foreign visitors and merchants were welcomed, commerce was conducted, and those with experience in negotiating transactions or disputes between individuals or groups – the wise – were also to be found. Wisdom acted as the accepted international language of human dealings, whether royal or common, commercial or philosophical. It was universally understood as the glue that bound ancient Near Eastern nations together.[16]

The post-exilic biblical writers believed that the exile came about because of the intrinsic conflict between the Davidic kingship's need for self-preservation and the prophetic insistence on relying only on the divine word for authority and protection. They envisioned a new Israel ruled directly by God by pure application of the divine *torah* through perfect divine wisdom, as implied by Jeremiah 31:31-34, quoted above. Because such a new Israel would encompass members who were scattered far and wide by the exile, wisdom rather than law was a natural choice for the biblical authors of a universal medium through which God's *torah* could reach exiles scattered throughout the nations. More than that, however, wisdom became the medium whereby the nations could themselves be invited to implement the scriptural imperative to seek the good of outsiders and bring them to knowledge of God's saving *torah*. And the nations' acceptance of this invitation would bring the rest of the world into the observance of God's word, and thus into the fulfillment of the universal implications of God's covenants with Abraham and, later, with the people in exile.

That the wisdom writings of the Old Testament were Israel's attempt to proclaim the biblical message to its neighbors in a language all could understand – i.e, to tie the *hokmah* those nations sought to God's *torah* itself – can be seen in the Greek prologue to the Wisdom of Sirach.[17] In it, the author mentions the "high necessity" of providing those who did not know Hebrew, yet "who wished to gain learning, being prepared in character to live according to the law," a translation of those writings into Greek, the common language of the Eastern Mediterranean after Alexander the Great. The phrase "instruction and wisdom" occurs twice in this passage, obviously bringing together the key words *torah* and *hokmah* to link them in the mind of listeners.

> [H]e who devotes himself to the study of the law of the Most High will seek out the wisdom of all the ancients, and will be concerned with prophecies; he will preserve the discourse of notable men and penetrate the subtleties of parables; he will seek out the hidden meanings of proverbs and be at home with the obscurities of parables. He will serve among great men and appear before rulers; he will travel through the lands of foreign nations, for he tests the good and the evil among men. He will set his heart to rise early to seek the Lord who made him, and will make supplication before the Most High; he will open his mouth in prayer and make supplication for his sins. If the great Lord is willing, he will be filled with the spirit of understanding; he will pour forth words of wisdom and give thanks to the Lord in prayer. He will direct his counsel and knowledge aright, and meditate on his secrets. He will reveal instruction in his teaching, and will glory in the law of the Lord's covenant. (Sir 39:1-8)

Here, Sirach deliberately placed torachically-oriented

wisdom on a par with the Torah and Prophets, making it a legitimate candidate for scriptural status. The eventual canonization of the Wisdom Writings allowed the introduction of an essential third perspective into the Old Testament. Both Torah and Prophets address Israel; that is, they address the inside, in form if not in content, and could be mistakenly used to justify attitudes of "chosenness." But the Writings, which are addressed to outsiders in a language understood universally, insist anew that the Torah and Prophets are part of God's master plan to restore all peoples to himself through fulfillment of the covenant with Abraham. Without the Writings, post-exilic Israel would not be bringing God's word to the nations, but rather bringing the nations into Israel's word.

By its nature as well as its content, wisdom in the Old Testament shores up the purpose of the Torah and Prophets in proclaiming God's blessing to all nations. But the invitation to the Gentiles carries with it the same condition to which Israel is also subject: one will be included in God's chosen nation, yes, but only by abiding by the rules of the life-giving *torah*. And since the *torah* demands that one look outside oneself to the poor and oppressed, the widow and the orphan, the stranger and sojourner, then the ultimate test of membership in the covenant is whether one is caring for the needy neighbor, even if outsider. We the believers who are from all nations and have become the new Israel of God (Gal 6:16) must understand that our vocation is bound by the demands of *torah* – the demands which, according to St. Paul, boil down to love of the neighbor. Whatever our "career" is, this love must be our vocation.

"Christ, the Wisdom of God"

The Old Testament's development of universal wisdom into an invitation to embrace God's law forms the background for a striking passage from 1 Corinthians, in which St. Paul sharply distinguishes worldly wisdom from divine wisdom and identifies Jesus himself as "the wisdom of God":

> For Christ did not send me to baptize but to preach the gospel, and not with eloquent wisdom, lest the cross of Christ be emptied of its power. For the word of the cross is folly to those who are perishing, but to us who are being saved it is the power of God... For consider your call, brethren; not many of you were wise according to worldly standards, not many were powerful, not many were of noble birth; but God chose what is foolish in the world to shame the wise, God chose what is weak in the world to shame the strong, God chose what is low and despised in the world, even things that are not, to bring to nothing things that are, so that no human being might boast in the presence of God. He is the source of your life in Christ Jesus, whom God made our wisdom, our righteousness and sanctification and redemption; therefore, as it is written, "Let him who boasts, boast of the Lord." When I came to you, brethren, I did not come proclaiming to you the testimony of God in lofty words or wisdom. For I decided to know nothing among you except Jesus Christ and him crucified. And I was with you in weakness and in much fear and trembling; and my speech and my message were not in plausible words of wisdom, but in demonstration of the Spirit and of power, that your faith might not rest in the wisdom of men but in the power of God. Yet among the mature we do impart wisdom, although it is not a wisdom of this age or of the rulers of this age, who are doomed to pass away. But we impart a secret and hidden wisdom of God, which God decreed before the ages for our

glorification. (1 Cor 1:17-18; 1:26-2:7)

For St. Paul, the "wisdom of God," which lies in the "word" of scripture,[18] is offered mainly to the weak and powerless among the nations just as the prophetic word brought solace to the poor, meek, and downtrodden in Israel. Christ crucified, the exemplar of the weak and powerless, can have nothing to do with the wisdom of this world, which by necessity must sacrifice the powerless for the sake of society's continuation.[19] But what is cast out by the world is taken up and given life by God.[20] The covenant promised in the Old Testament is fulfilled in a manner which can only come from God, not from the world. Those who hear his word and follow his instruction are at once encouraged and rebuked by the wisdom of the cross: encouraged, because the cross reminds the believer of the world's ultimate inability to nullify God's love; rebuked, because to follow Christ's example of love for the neighbor may demand nothing less than death – social, even physical – at the world's hands. Christ is the obedient servant of the *torah* and God's *dabar* in the Prophets, the one who understands that only service to the neighbor can make one a wise servant who is eligible for citizenship in God's kingdom.

Conclusion

What, then, may be learned from the Old Testament about Christian vocation? Simply put, that any Christian definition of vocation must be rooted not only in the Old Testament's understanding of God's insistent call to his people to fulfill his *torah* in the sight of the rest of the world, but also that any temptation to turn inward towards the security of excluding others must be shunned as direct rebellion against God. To seek the good of the other is wise; to seek only our own good, unwise.

The entire Bible teaches us that we are called to assist our needy neighbor without regard to whether they are Christian or pagan, inside the Church or outside it, appealing or repulsive, acceptable or unacceptable in society. Vocation is not a matter of choosing among our inner aptitudes or personal preferences, but of responding to God's call to care for the weak and defenseless. Like ancient Israel, which was once a sojourner in the land of Egypt, we are instructed by our Lord through his Word to lead our neighbor into the kingdom which is God's and not ours.

The "conventional" wisdom of our time, which in Western and especially American culture bases itself on self-fulfillment, urges us to "follow our dreams," and "do what we love." Even the churches have picked up on this line of thought, so that "personal growth in Christ" and "unlocking our spiritual potential" have become watchwords for "discerning" our callings from God, not to mention the idea that developing one's innate talents can be equated with one's Christian vocation. But these approaches focus inward on the self, not outward to the neighbor. God's gifts come from God, not from oneself, and are made by God according to current needs. None of the prophets or apostles were careerists. As we know from the stories of their calling, many of them vigorously protested their calling by God. Indeed, how can prophecy or apostleship or any of the spiritual gifts mentioned by St. Paul in 1 Corinthians 12 derive from inborn talents or self-fulfillment? And if somehow they do, how then can their exercise by believers be a truly loving response to the needs of others without even the faintest taint of self-interest?

The Wisdom Writings, in the last analysis, push us beyond self-satisfaction among our Christian friends to taking up the cross, practically as well as inwardly. As those who have been brought into the congregation of those who heed God's instruction, we are commanded to seek the good of the outsider and love our enemies, to go even beyond "loving those who hate us" to loving those we hate. This is to have the mind of Christ. If we do not pursue *his* mind as our first vocation, we stand no chance of having "a good answer before the dread judgment seat of Christ." Only the *debar yahweh*, "Christ the wisdom, word, and power of God," a teaching which was brought to us *by others* when we ourselves were outsiders and which we also must bring to outsiders, can provide us with such an answer.

Notes

1 Why must this "common mind" be necessarily communicated and taught (and not, for example, innate, just needing to be drawn out)? Taking the example of the passage quoted above, it is clear that Paul has to *teach* the necessity of looking to the interest of others, which he would not have to mention if the community was doing this naturally. In the biblical world, whether or not teaching *forms* the hearer or merely *draws out* what is naturally good in the hearer is irrelevant; what *is* relevant is that the teaching word is vital to the understanding of the hearer, since the teacher is equivalent to the father, they both form their progeny through the "word." See Gal 4:19-20 and 1 Cor 4:15-17.

2 Readers of Greek will appreciate the emphasis John uses to stress the divine nature of the Word: *kai theos hen o logos*.

3 John Chrysostom, *Isa Interp.*, 1.4.

4 John Chrysostom, *Isa Interp.*, 5.3.

5 Readers unfamiliar with the Old Testament should expect that they will have to read much of the ensuing paper slowly, and are

encouraged to simultaneously read and familiarize themselves with the biblical text itself.

6 "The Law" is comprised of the first five books of the Old Testament: Genesis, Exodus, Leviticus, Numbers, and Deuteronomy.

7 "The Prophets" is divided into two sections, the Former Prophets and the Latter Prophets. The Former Prophets includes Joshua, Judges, 1 and 2 Samuel, and 1 and 2 Kings (Samuel and Kings are referred to as "The Books of the Kingdoms" in the Septuagint). The Latter Prophets include Isaiah, Jeremiah, Ezekiel, and the Scroll of the Twelve Prophets. The Scroll of the Twelve Prophets includes Hosea, Joel, Amos, Obadiah, Jonah, Micah, Nahum, Habakkuk, Zephaniah, Haggai, Zechariah, and Malachi. Regarding the Scroll of the Twelve Prophets, traditionally they are considered as one book – even in the Septuagint they are referred to as *dodekapropheton*.

8 The Psalms and Wisdom Writings includes the Psalms, Lamentations, Song of Solomon (also known as Song of Songs), Proverbs, Job, Ecclesiastes, Ruth, Esther, Daniel, , Ezra and Nehemiah (known as I and II Esdras in Greek Bibles), and Chronicles. This grouping of books follows the order of the Hebrew Bible, rather than the order of the Septuagint.

9 In this paper "The Torah" refers technically to the first five books of the Old Testament; *torah* refers to the more general concept of instruction/teaching.

10 See Rom 1:22-23: "Claiming to be wise, they became fools, and exchanged the glory of the immortal God for images resembling mortal man or birds or animals or reptiles."

11 See especially the so-called first commandment of the Decalogue: "I am the Lord your God, who brought you out of the land of Egypt, out of the house of bondage. You shall have no other gods before me. You shall not make for yourself a graven image, or any likeness of anything that is in heaven above, or that is in the earth beneath, or that is in the water under the earth; you shall not bow down to them or serve them; for I the Lord your God am a jealous God, visiting the iniquity of the fathers upon the children to the third and the fourth generation of those who hate me, but showing steadfast love to thousands of those who love me and keep my commandments." (Exod 20:2-6/Deut 5:6-10).

12 "Hear the word which the Lord speaks to you, O house of Is-

rael. Thus says the Lord: 'Learn not the way of the nations, nor be dismayed at the signs of the heavens because the nations are dismayed at them, for the customs of the peoples are false. A tree from the forest is cut down, and worked with an axe by the hands of a craftsman. Men deck it with silver and gold; they fasten it with hammer and nails so that it cannot move. Their idols are like scarecrows in a cucumber field, and they cannot speak; they have to be carried, for they cannot walk. Be not afraid of them, for they cannot do evil, neither is it in them to do good.' There is none like thee, O Lord; thou art great, and thy name is great in might. Who would not fear thee, O King of the nations? For this is thy due; for among all the wise ones of the nations and in all their kingdoms there is none like thee. They are both stupid and foolish; the instruction of idols is but wood!" (Jer 10:1-8)

13 Jeremiah's complaint is classic: "O Lord, thou hast deceived me, and I was deceived; thou art stronger than I, and thou hast prevailed. I have become a laughingstock all the day; every one mocks me. For whenever I speak, I cry out, I shout, 'Violence and destruction!' For the word of the Lord has become for me a reproach and derision all day long. If I say, 'I will not mention him, or speak any more in his name,' there is in my heart as it were a burning fire shut up in my bones, and I am weary with holding it in, and I cannot." (Jer 20:8-9) So Amos' answer regarding his calling: "And Amaziah said to Amos, 'O seer, go, flee away to the land of Judah, and eat bread there, and prophesy there; but never again prophesy at Bethel, for it is the king's sanctuary, and it is a temple of the kingdom.' Then Amos answered Amaziah, 'I am no prophet, nor a prophet's son; but I am a herdsman, and a dresser of sycamore trees, and the Lord took me from following the flock, and the Lord said to me, Go, prophesy to my people Israel.'" (Amos 7:12-15)

14 The order in which the four books of Isaiah, Jeremiah, Ezekiel, and the Twelve Prophets appear in the Biblical canon follows the pattern A, B, B', A'. Isaiah (A) and the Twelve Prophets (A') are on the "outside" and encompass Jeremiah (B) and Ezekiel (B') that form the "inner" part of the pattern. This pattern is known in literature as *inclusio* (inclusion)."

15 See e.g. Isa 51:11: "And the ransomed of the LORD shall return, and come to Zion with singing; everlasting joy shall be upon their

heads; they shall obtain joy and gladness, and sorrow and sighing shall flee away."

16 For more detail see Paul Nadim Tarazi, *Old Testament Introduction;* vol.3: *Psalms and Wisdom,* St. Vladimir's Seminary Press, Crestwood, NY, 1996, 107-120.

17 The Prologue reads as follows: "Whereas many great teachings have been given to us through the law and the prophets and the others that followed them, on account of which we should praise Israel for instruction and wisdom; and since it is necessary not only that the readers themselves should acquire understanding but also those that love learning should be able to help the outsiders by both speaking and writing, my grandfather Jesus, after devoting himself especially to the reading of the law and the prophets and the other books of our fathers, and after acquiring considerable proficiency in them, was himself also led to write something pertaining to instruction and wisdom, in order that, by becoming conversant with this also, those who love learning should make even greater progress in living according to the law.

"You are urged therefore to read with good will and attention, and to be indulgent in cases where, despite our diligent labor in translating, we may seem to have rendered some phrases imperfectly. For what was originally expressed in Hebrew does not have exactly the same sense when translated into another language. Not only this work, but even the law itself, the prophecies, and the rest of the books differ not a little as originally expressed.

"When I came to Egypt in the thirty-eighth year of Euergertes and stayed for some time, I found opportunity for no little instruction. It seemed highly necessary that I myself should devote some pains and labor to the translation of the following book, using in that period of time great watchfulness and skill in order to complete and publish the book for those living abroad who wished to gain learning, being prepared in character to live according to the law."

18 Notice how Christ, who is the content of Paul's gospel, is cast in scriptural terminology: not only wisdom, but righteousness, sanctification, and redemption. Notice also how the invitation itself not to boast is a scriptural quotation. Notice finally that, in the original Greek, the phrase "the word of the cross" is *ho logos ho tou*

stavrou, whose meaning is "the word, i.e., the gospel, which has as its content the preaching of the cross, i.e., Christ crucified." In turn, this "word of preaching" is based on the "word" of Scripture, as is clear from the reference to Old Testament terminology (see also Rom 1:1-2 "Paul, a servant of Jesus Christ, called to be an apostle, set apart for the gospel of God which he promised beforehand through his prophets in the holy Scriptures, the gospel concerning his Son.")

19 Even that gospel's messengers themselves are "weak and foolish": "For I think that God has exhibited us apostles as last of all, like men sentenced to death; because we have become a spectacle to the world, to angels and to men. We are fools for Christ's sake, but you are wise in Christ. We are weak, but you are strong. You are held in honor, but we in disrepute. To the present hour we hunger and thirst, we are ill-clad and buffeted and homeless, and we labor, working with our own hands. When reviled, we bless; when persecuted, we endure; when slandered, we try to conciliate; we have become, and are now, as the refuse of the world, the offscouring of all things." (1 Cor 4.9-13)

20 "But we have this treasure in earthen vessels, to show that the transcendent power belongs to God and not to us. We are afflicted in every way, but not crushed; perplexed, but not driven to despair; persecuted, but not forsaken; struck down, but not destroyed; always carrying in the body the death of Jesus, so that the life of Jesus may also be manifested in our bodies. For while we live we are always being given up to death for Jesus' sake, so that the life of Jesus may be manifested in our mortal flesh. So death is at work in us, but life in you." (2 Cor 4.7-12)

Seek First His Kingdom:
An Invitation to Christian Vocation

John Barnet

Introduction

A number of years ago the abbot of a monastery answered my question of vocation – whether I should get married or become a monk – with the startling words, "God doesn't care." He then added, "God only cares that you seek first his kingdom."

The context of the abbot's words is, of course, the Sermon on the Mount in St. Matthew's Gospel. Jesus is instructing his disciples and the crowds on the power of God to provide for basic human needs, exhorting them not to be concerned about earthly security:

> Therefore I tell you, do not be anxious about your life, what you shall eat or what you shall drink, nor about your body, what you shall put on. Is not life more than food, and the body more than clothing? Look at the birds of the air: they neither sow nor reap nor gather into barns, and yet your heavenly Father feeds them. Are you not of more value than they? And which of you by being anxious can add one cubit to his span of life? And why are you anxious about clothing? Consider the lilies of the field, how they grow; they neither toil nor spin; yet I tell you, even Solomon in all his glory was not arrayed like one of these. But if God so clothes the grass of the field, which today is alive

43

and tomorrow is thrown into the oven, will he not much more clothe you, O men of little faith? Therefore do not be anxious, saying, "What shall we eat?" or "What shall we drink?" or "What shall we wear?" For the Gentiles seek all these things; and your heavenly Father knows that you need them all. But *seek first his kingdom* [italics added] and his righteousness, and all these things shall be yours as well. (Matt 6:25–33)

As you might imagine, my initial reaction to the abbot's words was disappointment. Although "vocation" is perhaps most often associated with a religious calling (whether to a lay or ordained ministry), it is also commonly used to refer to one's life's work, even simply one's occupation. I believed at the time that I was asking the right question: What did God want me to do with my life?

In the years that followed, I studied at seminary, got married, completed doctoral studies, and fathered two sons. Although I often recalled the abbot's words – "God only cares that you seek first his kingdom" – there remained the lingering suspicion that God had intended a special purpose for me that I had failed to discern. As I reflect on these words today, I realize now that the abbot had in fact answered my question. Indeed, all things – even knowledge of one's vocation – are provided to those who first seek God's kingdom.

Implicit in the abbot's scriptural admonition is an analogy between God's providential care and the disclosure of a divinely-appointed vocation. Just as the Father provides our basic human needs of food and clothing, by simple extension, so must he provide for our needs regarding our vocation in the world. And if we are not to be anxious about what we are to eat, to drink, or to wear because our heavenly Father will provide these things, so must we not be anxious about what we are to do. Indeed, as Jesus instructs his disciples, we are *not even to ask the questions* "What shall we eat?" or "What shall we drink?" or "What shall we wear?" If we recognize that these questions are simply variations of the question "What shall we do?", then we must face the notion that, according to Jesus, this kind of questioning is born out of anxiety and is not compatible with a life of discipleship. Regarding food, drink, clothing – and vocation – Jesus says clearly: seek first the Father's kingdom and his righteousness and all these things shall be yours as well.

In order to understand vocation in this sense, therefore, we must answer the following questions: What does it mean to seek God's kingdom? Why does Jesus exhort us not to be anxious? Does God call us for a special purpose? How does he reveal to us our vocation?

To answer these questions we should first ask: how do Orthodox Christians begin to answer such questions? The approach that I take in this essay – a close reading of Scripture, in particular St. Matthew's Gospel – is foundational for the Church, our common life of faith and the locus of our salvation. Indeed, as Fr. Thomas Hopko once explained, "Everything in the Church is judged by the Bible. Nothing in the Church may contradict it. Everything in the Church must be biblical; for the Church, in order to be the Church, must be wholly expressive of the Bible; or more accurately, it must be wholly faithful to and expressive of that reality to which the Bible is itself the scriptural witness."[1] It is my hope that by illuminating the scriptural witness my word about vocation will be faithful to our Orthodox tradition.

Seeking the Kingdom

What does it mean to seek God's kingdom? In the context of the Sermon on the Mount, to seek God's kingdom essentially means to seek his righteousness, as implied by the parallelism between "kingdom" and "righteousness" in Jesus' invitation to his followers: "But seek first his kingdom and his righteousness, and all these things shall be yours as well" (Matt 6:33). Although some scholars have argued that the righteousness of God connotes God's activity toward human beings, whether understood as the gift of a new covenant[2] or the end-time imposition of his kingdom and the vindication of his saints,[3] most commentators agree that righteousness here refers to the right conduct that God requires of disciples.[4] Why then does Jesus speak of *God's* righteousness in Matthew 6:33 and not the righteousness of disciples, as in Matthew 5:20? The most likely explanation is that it reminds the reader that divine righteousness serves as the norm of human activity and criterion of final judgment, and that the knowledge of this divine righteousness is itself a gift of God.[5] In this context, therefore, it can be argued that "kingdom" and "righteousness" are essentially interchangeable.[6]

To seek God's kingdom, which is his righteousness, means that one must first know God's will, for God's will is to be the norm of human conduct. While the mission of Jesus unquestionably is to "save his people from their sins" (Matt 1:21), a mission that is foreshadowed by his very name and ultimately accomplished by his voluntary death, the most prominent activity of Jesus during his ministry, as understood by Matthew, is teaching his followers the will of God. Uniquely characteristic of Matthew's Gospel is the grouping of Jesus' instruction into five blocks of material,[7] an arrangement that is reminiscent of the five books of the Pentateuch and suggestive of Jesus' role as the one greater than the lawgiver Moses.[8] In the Sermon on the Mount, the first of these blocks of instruction, Jesus discloses the will of God by repeatedly contrasting the written law or rabbinic interpretations of the law with his own interpretations:

> You have heard that it was said to the men of old, "You shall not kill; and whoever kills shall be liable to judgment." *But I say to you* [italics added] that every one who is angry with his brother shall be liable to judgment... (5:21–22)

> You have heard that it was said, "You shall not commit adultery." *But I say to you* [italics added] that every one who looks at a woman lustfully has already committed adultery with her in his heart. (5:27–28)

> It was also said, "Whoever divorces his wife, let him give her a certificate of divorce." *But I say to you* [italics added] that every one who divorces his wife, except on the ground of unchastity, makes her an adulteress... (5:31–32)

> Again you have heard that it was said to the men of old, "You shall not swear falsely, but shall perform to the Lord what you have sworn." *But I say to you* [italics added], Do not swear at all... (5:33–34)

> You have heard that it was said, "An eye for an eye and a tooth for a tooth." *But I say to you* [italics added], Do not resist one who is evil. (5:38–39)

> You have heard that it was said, "You shall love

your neighbor and hate your enemy." *But I say to you*
[italics added], Love your enemies and pray for those
persecute you… (5:43–44)

Although it is sometimes argued that the interpretations of Jesus represent an abrogation of the law, particularly in the matter of divorce, this seems unlikely
in light of Jesus' resolute insistence that his teaching
upholds the law: "Think not that I have come to abolish the law and the prophets; I have come not to abolish them but to fulfill them. For truly, I say to you, till
heaven and earth pass away, not an iota, not a dot, will
pass from the law until all is accomplished" (Matt 5:17–
18). More persuasive, therefore, is David Garland's explanation:

> Jesus restores [the law's] original intention. He does
> not add more laws nor raise the standards of what
> is right. Instead, he recovers what God has always
> required in the law – much like those who removed
> the accumulation of grime that collected over the years
> on Michelangelo's paintings in the Sistine Chapel in
> order to restore them to their full glory.[9]

A passage later in Matthew supports this interpretation that Jesus restores the original intention of the
law. In chapter 19, Jesus uses precisely the argument of
God's original intention to challenge the stance of the
Pharisees on the question of divorce:

> Have you not read that he who made them from the
> beginning made them male and female, and said, "For
> this reason a man shall leave his father and mother
> and be joined to his wife, and the two shall become
> one flesh"? So they are no longer two but one flesh.
> What therefore God has joined together, let not man
> put asunder. (Matt 19:4–6)

Although the Pharisees have framed their confrontation with Jesus as an exegetical debate on the valid grounds for divorce (cf. Deut 21:1–4), Jesus sidesteps the debate, instead upholding the law's original intention by interpreting its stipulations on divorce as a concession to human weakness: "[Jesus] said to them, 'For your hardness of heart Moses allowed you to divorce your wives, but from the beginning it was not so'" (Matt 19:8). Seeking the kingdom of God, therefore, is knowing the will of God; this will of God is revealed by Jesus, who in his teaching uncovers the original intention of God's law.

Yet to seek God's kingdom is not simply a matter of *knowing* the will of God; one must also *do* his will. When Herod the king assembles the chief priests and scribes to learn where the Christ is to be born, they correctly determine from the Scriptures, the repository of God's will, that he is to be born in Bethlehem (Matt 2:4–6). Herod subsequently uses this knowledge, however, to attempt to destroy the child (Matt 2:16) rather than to worship him (Matt 2:8, 11). On another occasion, Herod is confronted by John the Baptist, known to Herod and the people to be a prophet (Matt 14:5). The issue John the Baptist raises is the king's relationship with his sister-in-law. Despite the clear evidence of God's will on the matter of forbidden sexual relations, revealed both in the written law (Lev 18:16; 20:21) and the prophetic word of the Baptist, Herod refuses to act rightly, instead imprisoning (and subsequently executing) the prophet: "For Herod had seized John and bound him and put him in prison, for the sake of Herodias, his brother Philip's wife; because John said to him, 'It is not lawful for you to have her'" (Matt 14:3–4). Thus, the knowledge of God's will, though absolutely essential, is not sufficient. One must also accomplish his will, as Jesus himself insists regarding his own teaching: "Every one then who hears these words of mine *and does them* [italics added] will be like a wise man who built his house upon the rock" (Matt 7:24).

The portrayal of Herod represents a particularly egregious example of a Jewish leader who knows the will of God but refuses to do it. A more subtle form of disobedience, according to Matthew, is that of the Pharisees, religious contemporaries of Jesus who were known for their careful interpretation of the law.[10] One can detect – even in the harshly critical portrayal of the Pharisees in Matthew's Gospel (Matt 15:1–9; 23:4–36) – evidence of their remarkably meticulous observance of the law: "Woe to you, scribes and Pharisees, hypocrites! for you tithe mint and dill and cummin, and have neglected the weightier matters of the law, justice and mercy and faith; *these you ought to have done* [italics added], without neglecting the others" (Matt 23:23; cf. Lev 27:30). In short, despite the impression one gets from Matthew's Gospel that the Pharisees were, in Garland's words, "monstrous hypocrites," it is more likely that their righteousness "must have been popularly regarded as exceptional."[11] Therefore, to characterize their righteousness as insufficient – as Jesus implicitly does when he warns the crowds and his disciples that the kingdom requires of them a righteousness that "exceeds that of the scribes and Pharisees" (Matt 5:20) – would almost certainly have unsettled his listeners.[12]

To seek God's kingdom, therefore, means to perform the righteousness that exceeds that of the scribes and Pharisees, who despite their extraordinary attentiveness to the details of the law fall short of the right conduct required by God. The failing of the Pharisees

– and one of the reasons that their righteousness is un-acceptable to God – is that their conduct, which out-wardly appears to be good, in fact conceals iniquity within. One of the charges against the Pharisees – that they cleanse the outside of cups and plates[13] while ignoring the extortion and selfishness within (Matt 23:25–26) – metaphorically points to a discrepancy between appearance and reality, between the outside and the inside, between the Pharisees' actions and their heart[14] as their root problem. This character flaw of the Pharisees – of the inside failing to correspond to the outside – is directly attacked by Jesus when he com-pares the Pharisees to whitewashed tombs:[15] "Woe to you, scribes and Pharisees, hypocrites! for you are like whitewashed tombs, which outwardly appear beauti-ful, but within they are full of dead men's bones and all uncleanness. So you also outwardly appear righteous to men, but within you are full of hypocrisy and iniqui-ty" (Matt 23:27–28). The righteousness of the Pharisees, in other words, despite its apparent acceptability, is ac-tually not righteousness at all. Therefore, to perform the righteousness that exceeds that of the scribes and Pharisees means to perform actions that are not only outwardly good but also inwardly acceptable – the ac-tions, in other words, of a good and undivided heart.[16]

To define the root problem of the Pharisees simply as the failure of the inside to correspond to the outside, however, although essentially correct, is missing one element: the necessity of purity of intention. For ex-ample, one is inclined to accept the testimony of Paul the Pharisee that he excelled in Judaism (Phil 3:4–6), presumably because he was able to express faithfully the intention of his heart in acts of righteousness as de-fined by the law. Arguably, therefore, the hypocrites who sound a trumpet when giving alms (Matt 6:2) or pray on street corners (Matt 6:5), although rightly condemned by Jesus, do intend to fulfill the ethical and religious requirements of the law. Their problem is that by drawing attention to themselves they show that their actions are motivated by another intention as well – the desire to be praised by others. Jesus warns the crowds and his disciples that this condition of divided loyalties betrays an anxious self-concern that is incompatible with the life of discipleship. Moreover, it effectively contradicts their very confession of faith: "No one can serve two masters; for either he will hate the one and love the other, or he will be devoted to the one and despise the other. You cannot serve God and mammon" (Matt 6:24).

The condition of being "'divided' in one's fealty to God," therefore, can be understood here as an "inner incongruity,"[17] rather than a failure of intentions corresponding to actions, or even of words corresponding to deeds. Indeed, the actions of a hypocrite, so defined, do correspond to intentions; the intentions, however, are not necessarily made explicit, either to the hypocrite himself or to others.[18] One can say, therefore, that the righteousness that exceeds that of the scribes and Pharisees is possible only for the disciple whose divided heart has been renewed or made whole, who manifests the singleness of purpose that is pronounced blessed by Jesus in the Beatitude: "Blessed are the pure in heart, for they shall see God" (Matt 5:8).

In short, to seek God's kingdom means to possess the understanding and intention of God himself, the very mind of God, and to perform corresponding acts of righteousness. Such acts of righteousness are, in a sense, not one's own but are those of God, as Jesus teaches in the Sermon on the Mount:

> You have heard that it was said, "You shall love your neighbor and hate your enemy." But I say to you, Love your enemies and pray for those who persecute you, so that you may be sons of your Father who is in heaven; for he makes his sun rise on the evil and on the good, and sends rain on the just and on the unjust. For if you love those who love you, what reward have you? Do not even the tax collectors do the same? And if you salute only your brethren, what more are you doing than others? Do not even the Gentiles do the same? You, therefore, must be perfect, as your heavenly Father is perfect. (5:43–48)

Providential Care

Many of us are likely to agree that to seek the intention of God and perform corresponding acts of righteousness is, or should be, the goal of all Christians. But then understandably we move on to more basic questions – What shall we eat and wear? What shall we do? In each case, the biblical answer is the same – Do not be anxious. We are not to be anxious, because, as Jesus declares, our heavenly Father knows what we need and will provide it (Matt 6:33). He knows, for example, that we need food and clothing. In the missionary discourse of Matthew's Gospel, Jesus instructs his disciples, who also need food and clothing, not to rely on their own resources but on the hospitality of those who will receive them and accept their message of the kingdom:

> These twelve Jesus sent out, charging them, "Go nowhere among the Gentiles, and enter no town of the Samaritans, but go rather to the lost sheep of the house of Israel. And preach as you go, saying, 'The

kingdom of heaven is at hand.' Heal the sick, raise the dead, cleanse lepers, cast out demons. You received without paying, give without pay. *Take no gold, nor silver, nor copper in your belts, no bag for your journey, nor two tunics, nor sandals, nor a staff; for the laborer deserves his food. And whatever town or village you enter, find out who is worthy in it, and stay with him until you depart* [italics added]. As you enter the house, salute it. And if the house is worthy, let your peace come upon it; but if it is not worthy, let your peace return to you. And if any one will not receive you or listen to your words, shake off the dust from your feet as you leave that house or town. Truly, I say to you, it shall be more tolerable on the day of judgment for the land of Sodom and Gomorrah than for that town." (Matt 10:5–15)

The vulnerability of these missionary disciples – those who paradigmatically seek first God's kingdom – is itself to be understood as a sign of God's providential care: they are truly helpless, but God himself will care for them. And indeed, God does provide them with food and clothing, but only through those who accept the word of the kingdom. When the word is rejected, on the other hand, as it will be (Matt 10:14), rejection simply becomes another opportunity for the disciples to bear witness to the gospel: "Beware of men; for they will deliver you up to councils, and flog you in their synagogues, and you will be dragged before governors and kings for my sake, to bear testimony before them and the Gentiles" (Matt 10:17–18). Therefore, the disciples are exhorted not to become anxious, not to succumb to the condition of divided loyalties. Rather, they are to remain focused on their one task, which is to proclaim the word of the kingdom: "When they deliver you up, do not be anxious how you are to speak or what you are to say, for what you are to say will be given to you in that hour; for it is not you who speak, but the Spirit of your Father speaking through you" (Matt 10:19–20). Remarkably, the consolation of the disciples who face hunger, persecution, even death for the sake of the gospel is not that they will be delivered from their distress – they will not be. Their consolation rather is that God himself will provide the words of their testimony. For this reason, they are not to be anxious.

We are also not to be anxious, because, as Jesus assures us, the suffering and failure of those who proclaim the gospel do not represent the failure of the gospel itself. Those who turn away the missionary disciples are held accountable for their actions on the day of judgment (Matt 10:14–15), when it is revealed that the encounter with the disciples represented not only an opportunity to care for needy strangers but also an invitation to enter the kingdom. It has generally been maintained that the criterion of judgment in the parable of the last judgment (Matt 25:31–46) – "the least of these my brethren" – is the poor and neglected of all the nations. More recently, however, some scholars have argued that "the least" should be regarded as the missionary disciples,[19] who have followed the instructions of Jesus not to rely on their own resources but to depend on those to whom they preach the gospel for their food and clothing. At the final judgment, it is revealed that those who cared for the vulnerable missionaries have in fact ministered to the Son of man, who is both universal judge and the content of the good news. By caring for the needy disciples, they are shown to have implicitly accepted the gospel message. By caring for the needy disciples, they have ministered to the Son of man: "Then the righteous will answer him,

'Lord, when did we see thee hungry and feed thee, or thirsty and give thee drink? And when did we see thee a stranger and welcome thee, or naked and clothe thee? And when did we see thee sick or in prison and visit thee?' And the King will answer them, 'Truly, I say to you, as you did it to one of the least of these my brethren, you did it to me'" (Matt 25:37–40). Therefore, having performed the righteousness that exceeds that of the scribes and Pharisees, they are pronounced blessed by the judge and invited into the kingdom. On the other hand, those who neglected the needy disciples have also implicitly rejected the word of the kingdom. Consequently, they are sent "into the eternal fire prepared for the devil and his angels" (Matt 25:41), thus realizing the terrible outcome in store for those who refuse to accept the missionary disciples and their message: "And if any one will not receive you or listen to your words, shake off the dust from your feet as you leave that house or town. Truly, I say to you, it shall be more tolerable on the day of judgment for the land of Sodom and Gomorrah than for that town" (Matt 10:14–15). We are not to be anxious, in other words, because the apparent failure of our human efforts does not invalidate the gospel. This is indeed good news.

We are also not to be anxious, as Jesus reminds us, because life is more than food and clothing more than the body (Matt 6:25). Indeed, the ultimate expression of God's providential care is not that he provides for our material needs but that he provides his word as food and clothing, the means by which he renews a divided heart and makes possible the righteousness that exceeds that of the scribes and Pharisees. When Jesus, after having fasted for forty days in the wilderness, is tempted by the devil to change stones into bread in order to satisfy his hunger, he rebukes the devil, testifying that his food is the word of God: "It is written, 'Man shall not live by bread alone, but by every word that proceeds from the mouth of God'" (Matt 4:4; cf. Deut 8:3). In his response to the devil, Jesus exemplifies the singleness of purpose that is characteristic of an undivided heart. In the parable of the wedding feast (Matt 22:1–14), on the other hand, one of the guests is cast out of the feast because he is not wearing the proper clothing – a wedding garment: "But when the king came in to look at the guests, he saw there a man who had no wedding garment; and he said to him, 'Friend, how did you get in here without a wedding garment?' And he was speechless. Then the king said to the attendants, 'Bind him hand and foot, and cast him into the outer darkness; there men will weep and gnash their teeth.' For many are called, but few are chosen" (Matt 22:11–14). The several hyperbolic elements of the parable – killing of messengers, destruction of the city, indiscriminate invitation, harsh treatment of the unworthy guest – support the interpretation that more is intended here than a cautionary tale about proper wedding attire. Rather, as many commentators have observed, the parable is an allegory of the history of salvation and final judgment.[20] The wedding garment in particular denotes the works of righteousness required of those who have accepted the invitation of the kingdom, understood not as works meriting salvation but as works evidencing God's righteousness.[21] Works of righteousness are evidence of God's prior activity, however, only if they correspond to a renewed heart,[22] the true object of God's providential care, who graciously bestows his word as food and clothing.

Finally, we are not to be anxious because anxiety,

whether about the cares of the world or in the face of persecution, makes the word unfruitful, as the allegorical interpretation of the parable of the sower makes clear:

> Hear then the parable of the sower. When any one hears the word of the kingdom and does not understand it, the evil one comes and snatches away what is sown in his heart; this is what was sown along the path. As for what was sown on rocky ground, this is he who hears the word and immediately receives it with joy; yet he has no root in himself, but endures for a while, and when tribulation or persecution arises on account of the word, immediately he falls away. As for what was sown among thorns, this is he who hears the word, but the cares of the world and the delight in riches choke the word, and it proves unfruitful. As for what was sown on good soil, this is he who hears the word and understands it; he indeed bears fruit, and yields, in one case a hundredfold, in another sixty, and in another thirty. (Matt 13:18–23)

The word of the kingdom, which is offered indiscriminately to both the good and the bad alike (cf. Mat 22:10), not unexpectedly provokes responses of uncomprehending rejection and fruitful reception: earlier, Jesus had warned his disciples that their message would be rejected by some and accepted by others (Matt 10:11–15). Surprisingly, however, there are also some who will receive the word of the kingdom immediately and with joy, yet whose anxiety – the expression of a divided heart – will cause the word to be unfruitful, the very condition of those who reject the word outrightly. Arguably, the posture of unbelievers is even preferable to that of anxious believers – they at least do not (wrongly) perceive themselves as fruitful receivers of the word, they at least can still be confronted by their unbelief and possibly be saved (cf. Rev 3:15–16). Fruitful reception, therefore, the condition wherein works of righteousness correspond to a renewed heart, is possible only when one's loyalties are not divided, when neither worldly cares nor the fear of persecution distract one from the single-minded pursuit of God's kingdom. Blessed, indeed, are those who seek the kingdom of God with a pure heart.

A Special Calling

Does God call us for a special purpose? If by "special purpose" we mean marriage, a particular job, even a calling to ministry, then the answer is "no." As the abbot once remarked, "God doesn't care." God doesn't care because all vocations, as the Apostle Paul would have said, are "lawful" (cf. 1 Cor 10:23). God doesn't care because all vocations, in a sense, have been blessed.[23] The word of the kingdom is preached indiscriminately to show not only that good and bad alike are invited to enter the kingdom (cf. Mat 22:10), but also that the kingdom is offered to rich and poor, slave and free, Jew and Gentile, male and female, in other words, to all human beings of every social status and occupation (cf. Gal 3:28; Col 3:11), essentially sanctioning these social roles and occupations. In his letter to the Ephesians, for example, Paul instructs the various members of the household to pattern their lives after Christ's obedience and sacrificial love (Eph 5:21–6:9). It is noteworthy that Paul does not question the legitimacy of slavery, which at the time was not only the dominant social and economic institution of the Roman Empire but also arguably the most oppressive. Masters are not asked to release their slaves; slaves are not encouraged to seek their freedom. Rather, Paul reminds both masters and slaves that their relationship is to be informed by the example of Christ:

> Slaves, be obedient to those who are your earthly masters, with fear and trembling, in singleness of heart, as to Christ; not in the way of eye-service, as men-pleasers, but as servants of Christ, doing the will of God from the heart, rendering service with a good will as to the Lord and not to men, knowing that whatever good any one does, he will receive the same again from the Lord, whether he is a slave or free. Masters, do the same to them, and forbear threatening, knowing that he who is both their Master and yours is in heaven, and that there is no partiality with him. (Eph 6:5–9)

Paul's instructions have the effect of transforming slavery into a positive metaphor of life in Christ, challenging his readers to view an institution of oppression and exploitation as an opportunity for Christian witness.[24] While modern readers are often dismayed that Paul did not apparently take a stand against slavery, the point here is not to condone a social injustice.[25] Rather, the aim is to argue that the overriding intention of Paul is to articulate the possibility of Christian witness in every stratum of society. More often than not, we today are faced with a choice of vocations rather than being forced into an occupation not of our choosing. Nevertheless, the possibility of witness is the same in both situations. From this perspective one can say that all vocations – marriage, monasticism, investment banking, carpentry, teaching, medicine, military service, ordination, professional sports, itinerant preaching – are indeed "lawful," since all vocations have the possibility of being transformed into a positive image of life in Christ.

While it is true that all vocations are "lawful," it is also true that not all vocations are "helpful." All vocations are "lawful," but some vocations – those ostensibly at odds with a biblical ethos – prove more difficult than others to transform into an image of life in Christ. The rich man in Matthew's Gospel, for example, is unable to enter God's kingdom, despite faithfully observing all the commandments (Matt 19:16–22). Because he is unwilling to exchange his great possessions for a heavenly treasure, "he becomes a sign of how difficult it is for a rich man to enter the kingdom, much to the astonishment of the disciples, who apparently hold the view that property is a sign of God's favor: 'Who then can be saved' (Matt 19.25)? And like the rich man, many of us also turn away from this invitation [to sell what we have, give to the poor, and follow Christ], whether our possessions are many or few, before we understand the meaning of Jesus' words: 'With men this [salvation] is impossible, but with God all things are possible' (Matt 19.26)."[26] All vocations are "lawful," but some vocations prove unfruitful because we forget that they too must be animated each day by the spirit of Christian charity. In this regard it is important to recognize that the vocations that seem to match well with the life of service envisioned by the Bible, such as ministry, medicine, teaching, and so on, can be the ones we most forget need to be illuminated by this Christian charity.

In his letter to the Corinthians, Paul upholds the believers in Corinth who have correctly grasped the concept of Christian liberty, in this case, their right to eat meat offered in sacrifice to idols. Nevertheless, he also admonishes them for failing to understand that their newfound liberty in Christ is intended only for the purpose of building up of the community: "'All things are lawful,' but not all things are helpful. 'All things are lawful,' but not all things build up. Let no one seek his own good, but the good of his neighbor" (1 Cor 10:23–24). To seek one's own good at the expense of the neighbor, especially if it causes the neighbor to stumble, is to sin against Christ, as Paul warns the Corinthians (cf. 1 Cor 8:12). To seek one's own good at the expense of the neighbor is to act from a divided heart, the condition of anxious believers, who make the word of the kingdom unfruitful and thus are condemned on the day of judgment (cf. Mat 7:21–23). To seek the neighbor's good, on the other hand, to build up the neighbor even at the expense of one's own freedom in Christ, is to actualize the saving pattern of Jesus' kenosis, "who, though he was in the form of God, did not count equality with God a thing to be grasped, but emptied himself, taking the form of a servant, being born in the likeness of men. And being found in human form he humbled himself and became obedient unto death, even death on a cross" (Phil 2:5–8). To seek the neighbor's good at one's own expense, in other words, is to have the mind of Christ, a sign that the word of the kingdom has indeed been fruitful. All vocations, therefore, are "lawful," but only insofar as they are used to build up the community of believers. All vocations are "lawful," but only those that seek the neighbor's good are "helpful."

Does God call us for a special purpose? If by "special purpose," on the other hand, we mean a life of witness that informs all vocations, then the answer is "yes." Indeed, we Christians have only one true vocation – to witness to the salvation that God has accomplished in us. This vocation is strikingly depicted in the parable of the unforgiving servant (Matt 18:21–35), who is released by the king from the impossible debt of ten thousands talents for no reason other than that he pleads for mercy. Subsequently, the servant is expected to witness to his "salvation" by showing the same mercy to others. When he refuses to forgive a fellow servant the insignificant sum of a hundred denarii, however, his forgiveness is withdrawn and the servant is cast into prison. The lesson of the parable is clear: "So also my heavenly Father will do to every one of you, if you do not forgive your brother from your heart" (Matt 18:35). In the Sermon on the Mount, Jesus likens the witness of salvation to a light that shines before others: "You are the light of the world. A city set on a hill cannot be hid. Nor do men light a lamp and put it under a bushel, but on a stand, and it gives light to all in the house. Let your light so shine before men, that they may see your good works and give glory to your Father who is in heaven" (Matt 5:16). To perform good works openly before others, however, risks bringing praise to oneself rather than the glory to God. Indeed, the good works of the hypocrites are rejected by God because their intention is to secure the praise of others (Matt 6:1–5), the condition of a divided heart. The light of salvation, on the other hand, is none other than the word of the kingdom, which not only sustains the afflicted messenger of the gospel but also ascribes the messenger's works to the power of God:

> For what we preach is not ourselves, but Jesus Christ as Lord, with ourselves as your servants for Jesus' sake. For it is the God who said, "Let light shine out of darkness," who has shone in our hearts to give the light of the knowledge of the glory of God in the face of Christ. But we have this treasure in earthen

vessels, to show that the transcendent power belongs to God and not to us. We are afflicted in every way, but not crushed; perplexed, but not driven to despair; persecuted, but not forsaken; struck down, but not destroyed; always carrying in the body the death of Jesus, so that the life of Jesus may also be manifested in our bodies. For while we live we are always being given up to death for Jesus' sake, so that the life of Jesus may be manifested in our mortal flesh. (2 Cor 4:5–11)

The Scriptural Mind

How does God reveal to us our vocation? God reveals our vocation by transforming our hearts, the seat of our understanding and intention. God reveals our vocation, in other words, by giving us a scriptural mind.

Some fifty years ago Fr. Georges Florovsky bemoaned the Orthodox Christian's clear loss of the scriptural mind, despite our retaining "some bits of biblical phraseology." The biblical idiom had become archaic for the modern man, its relevance no longer a certainty. Fr. Georges expressed concern that our continuous process of reinterpretation, which he equated with the project of demythologizing Scripture, risked losing "the uniqueness of the Word of God." Instead, Florovsky asked,

> Would it not be safer to bend our thought to the mental habits of the biblical language and to relearn the idiom of the Bible? No man can receive the gospel unless he repents – "changes his mind." For in the language of the gospel "repentance" (*metanoeite*) does not mean merely acknowledgment of and contrition for sins, but precisely a "change of mind" – a profound change of man's mental and emotional attitude, an integral renewal of man's self, which begins in his

self-renunciation and is accomplished and sealed by the Spirit.[27]

Certainly, we today should use whatever tools we have at our disposal to identify our talents and our interests, and to match them to the needs of the world. Certainly, we should seek the advice of wise elders and discerning peers to help us discover our true calling, the one we are best suited for. Certainly, we should make the prayer of Jesus in Gethsemane – "not as I will, but as thou wilt" (Matt 26:39) – our daily petition, continuously framing our search for vocation in its proper context. But above all we should learn "to bend our thought to the mental habits of the biblical language" so that we might not only remind ourselves but also teach others that the most immediate question – What shall I do? – is not yet the most important one. The most important question is rather: How shall I witness in whatever I do?

I would like to conclude with a practical suggestion. While all vocations may indeed be "lawful" – and this must be affirmed – I am certain that unless one first seeks the kingdom of God, unless one first acquires the scriptural mind, not all vocations are "helpful." To acquire the scriptural mind, however, is not simply a matter of memorizing scriptural verses or faithfully attending divine services during Lent. Rather, to acquire the scriptural mind is a long process that begins with a daily encounter with God's word, not unlike the encounter that was prompted by our question of vocation. Not unexpectedly, the world is inhospitable to those who would acquire the scriptural mind, refusing to allow us the time in our normal lives to study, to pray, to reflect, and finally to repent. We need time for these activities to become an everyday part of our lives. Therefore, I propose that before anyone would answer the question of vocation, he or she should undertake a serious program of post-baptismal catechesis at a seminary, preferably for a year or two. While the formal requirements of a degree program may seem like an unnecessary concession to the ways of this world, still I can think of no better place (outside of a monastery) to begin a life of study, prayer, and reflection in community, without which the biblical language remains merely an archaic idiom and a life of witness the vocation only of saints.

Notes

1 Thomas Hopko, "The Bible in the Orthodox Church," in *All the Fulness of God: Essays on Orthodoxy, Ecumenism, and Modern Society* (Crestwood, NY: St. Vladimir's Seminary Press, 1982), 49–50.

2 Robert A. Guelich, *The Sermon on the Mount* (Waco, TX: Word Books, 1983), 84–87.

3 Robert H. Gundry, *Matthew: A Commentary on His Literary and Theological Art* (Grand Rapids, MI: Eerdmans Publishing, 1982), 118.

4 For example, W. D. Davies and Dale C. Allison, Jr., *A Critical and Exegetical Commentary on the Gospel According to Saint Matthew*, 3 vols. (Edinburgh: T&T Clark, 1988), 1:661; Dan O. Via, Jr., *Self-Deception and Wholeness in Paul and Matthew* (Minneapolis: Fortress Press, 1990), 85.

5 In the parable of the last judgment (Matt 25:31–46), the reader learns what is revealed to the sheep and the goats only when it is too late – that the care or neglect of the least is in fact the care or neglect of Jesus, who is thus both criterion of judgment and universal judge.

6 This is argued by W.D. Davies and Dale Allison, *Saint Matthew*, 1:661. "Righteousness is the law of the realm, the law of God's kingdom; and to participate even now in God's eschatological rule one must strive for the better righteousness of 5.20. Righteousness

is the narrow gate that leads to the life of God's kingdom. Thus, to seek the kingdom is to seek righteousness and to seek righteousness is to seek the kingdom."

7 Although the blocks of material, or "discourses," lack clear beginnings, they are generally defined roughly as follows: Sermon on the Mount (chs. 5–7); Missionary Discourse (ch. 10); Parables of the Kingdom (ch. 13); Discourse on Church Relationships (ch. 18); and Eschatological Discourse (chs. 23–25). See David R. Bauer, *The Structure of Matthew's Gospel: A Study in Literary Design*, Journal for the Study of the New Testament Supplement Series 31 (Sheffield: Almond Press, 1988).

8 See Dale C. Allison, Jr., *The New Moses: A Matthean Typology* (Minneapolis: Fortress Press, 1993).

9 David E. Garland, *Reading Matthew: A Literary and Theological Commentary on the First Gospel* (New York: Crossroad Press, 1993), 63.

10 The Apostle Paul, writing about his prior life as a Pharisee and persecutor of the church, leaves little doubt about his and his party's high regard for the law and its observance: "If any other man thinks he has confidence in the flesh, I have more: circumcised on the eighth day, of the people of Israel, of the tribe of Benjamin, a Hebrew born of Hebrews; as to the law a Pharisee, as to zeal a persecutor of the church, as to righteousness under the law blameless" (Phil 3:4–6). See also Josephus, *Jewish War* 1.110; 2.162.

11 Garland, *Reading Matthew*, 62.

12 One is reminded here of the disciples' astonishment – "Who then can be saved?" – upon being told by Jesus that "it is easier for a camel to go through the eye of a needle than for a rich man to enter the kingdom of God" (Matt 19:24). The lesson is that human status and achievement, even apparent signs of God's privilege (cf. Gen 24:35; 26:12–13), are irrelevant before the kingdom.

13 Possibly related to Lev 11:31–32, which requires that a vessel be washed in the event that a dead "swarming thing" should render it impure. See E. P. Sanders, *Jewish Law from Jesus to the Mishnah: Five Studies* (London: SCM Press, 1990), 39, 199–205.

14 In the biblical idiom the heart represents the seat of human understanding and intention.

15 The practice of whitewashing tombs may have been intended to mark tombs so as to prevent inadvertent overshadowing, which

arguably would cause the person to contract corpse impurity. See Sanders, *Jewish Law*, 39.

16 It has often been argued that the Pharisees in Matthew's Gospel represent the members of Matthew's Church, who themselves appear outwardly righteous but are full of iniquity within. The evangelist's oblique accusation against the members of his own community recalls the word of the prophet Jeremiah, who challenged the leaders of Judah to repent despite their appearance of righteousness (Jer 7:1–15). Contemporary readers of Matthew's Gospel, therefore, are challenged to see that they themselves are like the Pharisees. See John A. Barnet, *Not the Righteous but Sinners: M. M. Bakhtin's Theory of Aesthetics and the Problem of Reader-Character Interaction in Matthew's Gospel*, Journal for the Study of the New Testament Supplement Series 246 (London: T&T Clark, 2003).

17 Jack Kingsbury's definition of hypocrisy. See Jack Dean Kingsbury, *Matthew as Story* (Philadelphia: Fortress Press, 2nd edn, 1988), 20.

18 David E. Garland, *The Intention of Matthew 23* (Leiden: E. J. Brill, 1979), 100–101, has concluded that the dominant meaning of hypocrisy in Matthew's Gospel is a type of self-deception rather than a conscious pretense to fool others.

19 See, for example, Garland, *Reading Matthew*, 243–45; John R. Donahue, *The Gospel in Parable: Metaphor, Narrative, and Theology in the Synoptic Gospels* (Philadelphia: Fortress Press, 1988), 120–23

20 For example, Garland, *Reading Matthew*, 220; Donahue, *The Gospel in Parable*, 94.

21 Gundry, *Matthew*, 439; Garland, *Reading Matthew*, 223.

22 Some scholars have argued that the wedding garment signifies repentance, which is the transformation or renewal of the heart. See Craig S. Keener, *A Commentary on the Gospel of Matthew* (Grand Rapids, MI: Eerdmans Publishing, 1999), 522–23.

23 The point here is not to suggest that exploitative, demeaning, harmful "vocations," such as prostitution, drug-dealing, and so on, are blessed. Clearly, they are not. Rather, my provocative assertion is intended to challenge the thinking that there exists only a handful of "good" occupations suitable for life in Christ. The real challenge facing Christians, as I argue below, is how can we make our expression of a particular profession "good."

24 On the use of slavery as soteriological symbol, see Dale B. Martin, *Slavery As Salvation: The Metaphor of Slavery in Pauline Christianity* (New Haven: Yale University Press, 1990).

25 On the other hand, in his letter to Philemon, Paul does ask the master to accept his runaway slave Onesimus as a brother and no longer as a slave (Phlm 10–20). Would the writers of the New Testament have been opposed to the eradication of slavery? Not likely. See Richard B. Hays, *The Moral Vision of the New Testament: Community, Cross, New Creation: A Contemporary Introduction to New Testament Ethics* (San Francisco: HarperCollins, 1996), who shows how the New Testament can be used as a guide for contemporary ethics.

26 John Barnet, "Stewardship and the New Testament" in *Good and Faithful Servant: Stewardship in the Orthodox Tradition,* edited by Anthony Scott (Crestwood, NY: St. Vladimir's Seminary Press, 2003), 49.

27 Georges Florovsky, "The Lost Scriptural Mind," in *Bible, Church, Tradition: An Eastern Orthodox View* (Belmont, MA: Norland Publishing, 1972), 10.

"A Life Worthy of God:"
Vocation According to St. Paul

"For you know how, like a father
with his children, we exhorted each one
of you and encouraged you and charged
you to lead a life worthy of God,
who calls you into his own kingdom and glory."
1 Thessalonians 2:11-12

Introduction

A few introductory remarks may be helpful to the
discussion of our subject. By vocation or calling we
usually mean a summons to a particular task or course
of life, one especially accompanied by a deep sense of
conviction and/or divine inspiration. Vocation is very
different from employment, that is, merely having a
job or being engaged in an occupation to earn a living. The secular meaning of vocation is closer to that of
profession, signifying a public expression of conviction
and social service through a chosen career. Professions
are distinguished in that they ordinarily require spe-
cialized knowledge and extensive training. In St. Paul's
instance, as we shall see, we have a clear and distinct
case of vocation, a direct and personal summons from

God to preach the good news of Christ and the gift of new life in him. Of course, St. Paul's understanding of vocation would exclude neither professional training, since he himself was an educated man of his time, nor any ordinary job or occupation carried out in witness to God and service to others.

The discovery of vocation involves both internal and external factors. Two words in modern Greek that sound the same but mean different things are instructive in this regard. The word *klesis*, from the verb *kaleo* ("to call"), signifies a role or way of life summoned by something or someone from outside the self. This *klesis* could be from God, country, community, ideology, influential person, or urgent need in the world such as helping the homeless in our society. In contrast, the word *klisis*, from the verb *klino* ("to incline"), signifies a role or way of life chosen in the light of a person's own inclinations, aptitudes, and predilection, such as becoming a musician or a physicist. The implications of these two meanings, while at times discordant in practice, work out best when fully integrated for the attainment of a human being's highest degree of authenticity and personal fulfillment. The Apostle Paul himself perceived his ministry as an overwhelming call from God, rather than a result of his own personal predilections leading to "self-realization" in the modern sense. However, in his response to God's call, St. Paul put into eager and full use all his personal gifts and skills, reaching the highest levels of maturity and loving service to God and to others.

Vocation is a complex issue with numerous aspects having to do with the questions of "who, what, and how."[1] The question of "who" is about identity, character, personhood, true humanity in relation to others and the whole of life. The question of "the what" pertains to the discovery of one's specific calling as teacher, priest, monastic, musician, politician, or other, sometimes entailing overlapping vocations. The question of "the how" pertains to the principles, values, attitudes, and ways of conduct involved in the exercise of a chosen vocation. All three questions are closely related. Neither "the what" can be understood apart from "the who," nor "the who" apart from "the what," nor "the how" apart from both "the who" and "the what." The answers given to these questions determine each person's integrity, as well as the value of one's contribution to society. As we will see from the following discussion, the answers to these fundamental issues, according to St Paul, are astonishingly God-centered ("theocentric") and community-centered ("communal" or "corporate") in ways that many might find difficult to conceive in modern times.

The Question of Who to Be

Who are we called to be? Who or what calls us to be what we ought to be? If in my personal journey I search for a vocation in harmony with my true self, who am I? What is my true nature and destiny? What is human personhood? What is true humanity? How do I discover who I am that I might be true to my deepest self? What is my own self-understanding and on what terms do I aspire to make a meaningful contribution to society?

In the context of modern and postmodern North America, powerful factors largely predetermine how those queries are answered – based on democracy, individualism, procurement of goods, attainment of positions of wealth and distinction, and the pursuit of convenience and pleasure. Even as United States culture has shifted from modernism to postmodernism – that is, from an optimistic worldview of progress based on reason, science and technology to a pessimistic worldview of virtually chaotic relativism, pluralism and cultural wars – what still remains is the anthropocentric self as the measure of all things.[2] Because the prevailing social and intellectual currents often overshadow the deep questions of life, most people deal with the issue of "who to be" in the manner society dictates – in terms of individual rights, individual predilections, individual careers, individual satisfactions, and individual security necessitated by a seemingly disordered and confusing world. We may call this perspective an anthropocentric approach to vocation by which individuals create their own meaning and seek "self-realization" according to their personal judgment and good pleasure.[3] The end result may be that many "vocations" and "professions" in today's world are trivialized as masked pursuits of self-aggrandizement and/or personal enrichment for the maximum consumption of worldly goods and delights.[4]

St. Paul grew up in a religious culture with entirely different presuppositions centered on God and community. He tells us that, prior to his conversion experience, he lived proudly as a Hebrew of Hebrews, adhering devotedly to the law of Moses, one advanced in Judaism far beyond his contemporaries. He was exceedingly zealous about his religious traditions to the extent that he violently persecuted other Jews who had become Christians.[5] Of course not every Jew was fanatical like Paul. But all Jews shared an identity long established by community and heritage, centered on faith in God, the Mosaic law, the worship of the temple, the land, and Jewish corporate consciousness. The essentials of "who to be" were already set by the community defined by its vision of being the elect people of God, Creator and Ruler of the universe. God had covenanted with the Jewish people. His people were called to live in holiness and righteousness according to God's revealed laws and wisdom. Divine election and covenant, signifying a mutual bond of love and fidelity between God and his people, marked the essence of the religion of Judaism. The primary calling of every Jew was to love, worship, and obey God. "Hear, O Israel: The Lord is our God, the Lord alone;[6] and you shall love the Lord your God with all your heart, and with all your soul, and with all your might. And these words which I command you … you shall teach your children" (Deut 6:4-5).

From the standpoint of the Jewish tradition itself, God's blessings of election and covenant were never intended as racial prerogatives for the exclusive exaltation of the Jews. God's call to Israel entailed profound obligations. Israel was to be God's exemplary people and God's servant to all nations. Through Israel God desired to draw all people under his sovereign rule and righteousness – to bring his love, justice and peace to all the world. That was the idea behind God's great promise to Abraham that he would be the father of many nations and his descendants as numerous as the stars (Gen 15:5; 17:5; Rom 4:11-17). This universal vision of Israel as God's blessing to all nations finds its most powerful expression in the Book of Isaiah:

> I am the Lord, I have called you in righteousness,
> I have taken you by the hand and kept you,

I have given you as a covenant to the people,
a light to the nations (Isaiah 42:6).
I will give you as a light to the nations,
That my salvation may reach to the end of the earth.
(Isaiah 49:6b)[7]

Born in that religious and social context, St. Paul developed his primary sense of calling as a normal part of his growth in the Jewish community. His personal identity was formed by the corporate consciousness of the Jewish people. It is true that Jews of Paul's time differed, sometimes sharply, about how to interpret their elect status, their calling by God. Josephus, the first-century Jewish historian, famously reports several conflicting groups vying for influence. These were the Sadducees, the Pharisees, the Essenes, and the Zealots who sometimes did not shirk from murdering even fellow Jews perceived as collaborators with the Roman overlords.[8] All these factions were religiously based, for there was no facile distinction between religion and politics in ancient Judaism. Furthermore, the factions resulted not from abstract debates conducted in ivory towers. They were positions carved out by responses to the burning issues of the day, which in turn were influenced by a mix of political, religious, and economic realities in Palestine. Even among the Pharisees a diversity of opinion existed, from advocates of patience and peace to advocates of force and violence. Prior to his conversion, Paul belonged to the right wing of the religious and political spectrum. His ideals and purposes, as well as the consequent persecution of Jewish Christians, all were part of what he perceived to be his unwavering service to God.

Yet Paul the persecutor came to a dramatically new understanding of his calling on the road to Damascus.

Here is not the place for an analysis of the Damascus experience. Christian and Jewish scholars have interpreted the Damascus event not as a result of psychological tensions but as an objectively perceived religious experience in the Jewish religious tradition of epiphany or "theophany."[9] By "theophany" (literally, "manifestation of God") is meant a divine revelation in which the subject receives an extraordinary summons from God to fulfill a particular mission. Similar examples are the call of Moses (Exod 3:4-12), the call of Isaiah (Isa 6:1-8), and even the call of Jesus at the time of his baptism (Mark 1:9-11). The significance of such events lies not in psychological explanations, although psychological factors are not to be excluded, but in the implications of such experiences resulting in the transformation of personal lives and the perception of new insights about God, community, self, vocation, and the whole of reality.

For St. Paul the Damascus event was an about-face in that from zealous persecutor he turns into a fervent apostle of Jesus. Scholars debate whether the event should be interpreted as a "call" or "conversion." It was actually both. St. Paul viewed the event as a rare summons in the tradition of the call of the Old Testament prophets. Using the language of Isaiah and Jeremiah he writes: "When he [God] who had set me apart before I was born, and had called (*kalesas*) me through his grace, was pleased to reveal his Son to me…" (Gal1:15-16). St. Paul's vocation was to be a called (*kletos)* apostle of God and of Christ (Rom 1:1; 1 Cor 1:1). His was a call by the same God of Israel to a unique ministry as apostle to the Gentiles, to bring people from all nations under the rule and righteousness of God (Rom 11:13-14; Gal 2:1,7).

But the Damascus experience was also a conversion in the deepest personal terms. Paul the Pharisee came to new, transformed understanding of himself – "who he was" as a human being – and to a new vision of life. To be sure, his was not a conversion from sinner to righteous in the usual sense.[10] Paul was and always remained a faithful servant of God both before and after his conversion (Phil 3:5-16). His outlook continued to be theocentric and communal. Nor was it a conversion from one religion to another. What we call "Christianity" today was for him but the true and fulfilled Judaism. As he saw things, he was called to a specific task by the same God of Israel, the one true God who now was inaugurating a new world in Christ, calling both Jews and Gentiles to be his people. Yet the Damascus event was also most certainly a radical transformation of the Apostle's personal identity. Prior to his conversion, his whole life was centered on the Jewish law, of which he was a fanatical exponent. After his conversion, his life was focused on Christ whom he served with equal zeal – but entirely gone was the fanaticism and the violence.[11] Such was the radical change that, as an apostle of Christ, St. Paul could leave behind definitive aspects of Jewish life, for example, the requirements of circumcision, kosher foods, and the entire system of the Jewish law and temple, for a new personal and communal identity formed around the crucified and risen Christ, and embracing both Jews and Gentiles.

What inferences can we draw from our discussion of vocation thus far? One clear point is that the formation of vocation is significantly dependent on community. It is a truism to say that where communal identity is unified and strong, vocational calling is deeply formed as a matter of course within the community. Where community identity is weak, other factors in the broader culture take over. Just as important is the question of whether or not a community, a society, or a nation, has a coherent vision and truly lives by its professed principles and values. At issue is not the mere question about "what to be" in terms of a particular occupation or profession, but the more fundamental question of "who to be" as a community and as a member of a community in the wider context of life, before God and all people.

In the case of Orthodox Christians, our corporate identity is defined by our calling to be the One, Holy, Catholic, and Apostolic Church. Similar to the case of Judaism, this calling by God is not only a blessing but also an obligation – to be God's servants in the world. Yet, just as in the case of other religious communities, Orthodox Christians hold diverse views of their faith as they face multiple influences and challenges in contemporary society. Not unlike the religious groupings in St. Paul's time, Orthodox Christians practice several versions of their faith as they deal with the complex issues of their relationship to ethnic traditions, American acculturation, and the burdens of job and family. Sometimes the internal communal debate is not without tensions and the use of regrettable labels. At stake is the authenticity of the identity of the Church as the Church of God in her calling and mission to the world. Of course it should be understood that this fundamental issue – the formation of identity and vocation within the Church in harmony with its authentic nature and calling by God – is a matter that ought to concern the whole body of the Church. Although the leaders bear a special responsibility, all faithful according to Orthodox teaching are accountable for the state and direction of the Church.

The matter is too important to be conveniently left to a committee, a single project, or even an institution like a college or seminary. Defining communal and personal vocation within the Church are interdependent matters and decided by many factors, not least facing reality, truth-telling, listening to one another with mutual love and respect, as well as a large measure of humility and repentance before God, the ultimate source of calling and bar of accountability.

A second clear point from St. Paul's example is that identity and vocation cannot be authentically discovered apart from the quest after God, faithfulness to God, and the sincere seeking of God's will. St. Paul's quest led to the dramatic experience on the Damascus road, an event that not only defined his specific apostolic commission but also transformed his view of reality – God, the world, religion, life, true humanity, his very identity as a person. The Damascus event, at least in small measure, can be viewed as a powerful paradigm for the authentic search and discovery of one's true humanity and calling – both about "who to be" and about "what to be" with God's help. C. S. Lewis, the notable English literary figure, experienced something of a Damascus event while in deep meditation following the death of his wife. In postmodern America, Chuck Colson came to a rather sudden reversal of life and vision not long after the Watergate political scandal. Archbishop Anastasios of Albania, after serving many years in Africa, has worked a virtual miracle in the resurrection of the Church of Albania by his profound sense of calling and God's grace. Many examples in various religious communities could be cited as examples of extraordinary cases, testifying to what can properly be defined as true vocation – a calling that leads to the service of God and of others according to God's will.

Orthodox Christians need not wait for unexpected events or dramatic renewals. Their baptism is already a calling of "who to be" in the world. By virtue of their baptism and personal faith, Orthodox Christians enjoy a full share in God's election and covenant, God's summons to be his people, servants and examples to those willing to see and listen. The first task of the Orthodox Christian is to internalize this fundamental truth and then to allow it to flower to its fullest extent by God's grace. What is crucial is to work out "who to be" as an Orthodox Christian in order then to discern more clearly "what to be" and "how to be" in the presence of God and society. Orthodox Christians have invaluable opportunities through personal prayer and repentance, study and meditation, worship and stewardship, to experience periodic Damascus moments – moments of illumination, moments of conversion and self-knowledge, moments of renewal and empowerment for mission. The goal is to say with St. Paul: "It is no longer I who live but Christ who lives in me" (Gal 2:20). From such a theocentric and communal perspective, which offers vast possibilities of self-knowledge and spiritual maturity, Orthodox Christians can most effectively discover their true humanity, their calling in life, as well as responsible ways to critique, the life of the Church in order that the Church herself may stay on track in the fulfillment of her calling and mission in the world.[12]

The Question of What to Be

Although a traditional Jew, Paul was born a Roman citizen in the Hellenistic city of Tarsus, a center of edu-

cation, philosophy and culture.[13] He was a younger contemporary of Jesus but apparently never crossed paths
with him. He called himself *Pavlos,* the Greek form of
the Roman family name *Paulus* (meaning "small"). The
Book of Acts also refers to him as *Savlos,* the Greek form
of the Hebrew name *Saoul* or Saul (meaning "asked of
God"), but Paul himself never uses this name in his
letters. It was not unusual for Jews to take a second
name to testify to their roots. The two names of Paul,
and their variant etymological meanings, have nothing intentional to do with Paul's stature, personality, or
conversion.[14] However, his Roman and Greek cultural
backgrounds explain his facility in the use of the Greek
language and the ease with which he traveled around
the Mediterranean to carry out his commission as an
apostle of Christ.

Prior to his conversion Paul's own choice of "what to
be" was to join the strict religious faction of Pharisees,
a lay group devoted to the study and practice of the
Jewish Law. Choosing to be a Pharisee was for him the
most faithful way of responding to God's communal
call to all Israel. We do not know exactly why and how
he made that decision. No doubt it was partly because
of the influence of his traditional family (literally, "a
Hebrew from Hebrews," Phil. 3:5). Another reason
may have been his personal traits, gifted as he was
with the capacity for wholehearted commitment to a
cause. The Book of Acts reports that he studied with
Gamaliel (Acts 23:3), quite likely Gamaliel I, the Elder,
active in Jerusalem about 20-50 AD, and known for his
wisdom and moderation. Paul took a different path,
that of a fanatical Pharisee, making additional fateful
choices. He consented to the killing of St. Stephen the
Martyr (Acts 8:1). Soon after, by his own admission, he

turned to violent persecution of "the Church of God" (1 Cor 15:9; Gal 1:13-14). His precise activities as persecutor of other early Christians are not known. It appears that he was an authorized representative of the Jewish Council, bearing official documents, and seeking to punish Jewish Christians as far away as the synagogues in Damascus (Acts 9:1-2).[15] All this was part of the Jewish legal discipline under Roman law. It was also the context of Paul's most decisive experience in life, as already mentioned.

Although Paul chose to follow the path of a Pharisee, he did not "choose" in the same way to be an apostle of Christ. His call to be an apostle to the Gentiles was not a matter of personal considerations any more than the call of Moses to lead God's people out of Egypt, or the call of Isaiah to be a prophet. For the recipients of such extraordinary experiences, their calling was viewed as an obligation, a holy burden, placed in their innermost beings by God. In the words of the Prophet Amos: "The lion has roared; who will not fear? The Lord has spoken; who can but prophesy?" (Amos 3:8) And so it was with Paul. He writes: "Necessity is laid upon me. Woe to me if I do not preach the gospel" (1 Cor 9:16). His only choice in the matter was to carry out his commission gladly and free of charge, foregoing the apostolic right to get a living from the gospel, a joyful sacrifice that St. Paul esteemed a personal reward![16]

In certain respects, therefore, St. Paul's calling was an utterly unique case. It was not Paul's view that that there were many other apostles to the Gentiles. Although all Christians could freely spread the good news as occasion arose, and in spite of the fact that St. Paul always worked with a team of missionaries,[17] he conceived of his calling as a unique intervention of

God, an earmarking from his mother's womb, commissioning him to a task of worldwide and even cosmic implications. At least during the early years of the Christian movement, he was the acknowledged leader of the mission to the Gentiles just as Peter was the leader of the mission to the Jews (Gal 2:7-9). According to his own perception, he was given through God's call the enormous task of bringing in "the fullness of the Gentiles" according to God's plan. He contemplated that the success of his mission might well lead to the conversion of the "fullness of the Jews" and perhaps even usher in the consummation of all things with the glorious return of Christ and the resurrection of the dead (Rom 11:11-16, 25).

The extraordinary nature of St. Paul's vocation by no means precluded the Apostle's view that all Christians have a special calling. On the contrary, according to the Apostle, the gospel was a universal message of salvation, a call addressed to all people, inviting them to share equally the blessings of God's new revelation in Christ (2 Cor 5:17).[18] Having been given God's Spirit, God's power energizing the life of the early Church, all Christians were endowed with gifts and ministries. In two remarkable texts (1 Cor 12:4-31 and Rom 12:4-8), St. Paul envisions the Church as the body of Christ consisting of many members endowed with diverse gifts such as teaching, healing, prophesying, encouraging, giving, and administering. He mentions the chief ministries in a somewhat hierarchical order but without closing the list. "God has appointed in the Church first apostles, second prophets, third teachers, then workers of miracles, then healers, helpers, administrators, speakers in various kinds of tongues" (1 Cor 12:28). His point was the all Christians were gifted and all ministries had a particular role in the body of Christ. None was to be considered secondary or useless. All contributed to the well-being and edification of the community. The supreme gift for the harmonious function of all gifts was the gift of love about which the Apostle writes eloquently in 1 Cor 13.

How was a Christian to know what his particular calling by God was? St. Paul does not raise this question directly. He takes for granted that the Holy Spirit, palpably acting in the life of the Church, motivated and led Christians to express their particular gifts and fulfill their specific callings guided by love. In the context of a vibrant spiritual life it was up to each Christian to discern and contribute his gift to the building up of the life of the community. Here we must assume with the Apostle that the gifts of the Holy Spirit inevitably engaged the personality traits and the particular aptitudes of individuals, only now blessed, cleansed, illuminated, and directed by the experience of the new life in Christ. Proper discernment and practice of one's gifts could only come from the transformation of the Christian into a new creature in Christ. St. Paul's exhortation was that Christians should offer to God no longer dead animals as sacrifice but rather their very selves as "living sacrifice, holy and acceptable to God, which is your spiritual worship" (Rom 12:1). His admonition was equally striking: "Do not be conformed to this world but be transformed by the renewal of your mind, that you may prove what is the will of God, what is good and acceptable and perfect" (Rom 12:2). He counted that the new life in Christ, guided by the gift of love, would provide the understanding of "who to be" on the basis of which each Christian could then discern "what to be," that is, to discover his or her specific calling within the community of faith.

What about the relations of Christians to society, their jobs, professions, and ordinary contacts in pagan society? St. Paul was well aware of the necessities of life and the need to make a living. He himself worked with his hands, for a time in partnership with his close friends Aquila and Priscilla, all "tent-makers" or leather workers (Acts 18:2-3; 1 Cor 4:12; 1 Thess 2:9). The majority of the Christians belonged to the lower classes, "not many were powerful, not many were of noble birth" (1 Cor 2:26), consisting of small merchants, laborers, and not a few slaves. But some enjoyed higher social and economic status. Lydia, a leader of the Church of Philippi, ran a successful business (Acts 16:14). Philemon was a wealthy man who owned slaves (Phlm 16). Tertius was a professional scribe and Erastus was a city treasurer of Corinth, the Roman capital of Achaia at that time (Rom 16:22-23). Luke was a doctor (Col 4:14) and Zenas a lawyer (Titus 3:13). How were they to regard their calling as Christians within the Church and their obligations or professions in the pagan world?

The Apostle Paul did not expect that Christians should separate from society, but that they should shine as lights in the world.[19] He takes up the issue in an explicit way in 1 Corinthians 7:17-24 where he set down this principle: "Let everyone lead the life which the Lord has assigned him [in the world] and in which God has called him [to be a Christian]. This is my rule in all the churches" (1 Cor 7:17). For Paul, God's providence was responsible for the conditions and circumstances of all people in the world, each person having a status that in a general way could be considered a "call" by God (1 Cor 7:20). Even slaves who had become Christians did not need to be overly concerned about obtaining their freedom because in Christ they already possessed a true spiritual freedom.[20] Paul applied the same rule to marriage and single life, but did not prohibit persons from marrying, if they so fervently desired (1 Cor 7:25-40). The reason behind the Apostle's above fundamental principle is evident from the context. He expected the imminent return of Jesus from heaven and believed that in the remaining time a Christian ought to be wholly devoted to the Lord (1 Cor 7:29-32). What essentially mattered now was devotion to Christ and the life in Christ, not the ordinary jobs and conditions in which people found themselves. Christians were to live in the world "as if" they did not belong to the world, to "deal with the world as though they had no dealings with it. For the form of this world is passing away" (1 Cor 7:31). It was not that Christians were to abandon civic life and worldly responsibilities, but that they as God's elect people were to adopt a distinct, qualitative separation from the ways of the world, knowing where their true loyalties were. We see that Paul as a Christian continued to be governed by a strong theocentric and communal vision of life, now centered on Christ and the new community of the Church.

Let us now draw some further implications for our discussion on vocation pertaining to the question of "what to be" in the religious community and in society. A true story may serve as a striking illustration. Some years ago a seminarian was filled with anxiety over whether he should continue to seek the priestly calling or to pursue another profession. He sought advice from the late Bishop Gerasimos of blessed memory, a respected, Socrates-like figure. Upon speaking with the good bishop, the student was jolted receiving the following advice: "Do whatever you like, whatever comes your way, but do it well as a Christian. Whatever you choose, do it for the love of God and the service of others." At first the student was shocked and not a little offended by what appeared to be the bishop's insensitivity to the magnitude of his personal concern about a choice in life. However, he eventually realized how absorbed he was in his own self-centeredness and how appropriate the wisdom of that counsel was at that time. The bishop's advice was not far from what St. Paul might have said.

Today we live in a very different world from that of the Apostle. There are innumerable opportunities, at least in the developed world, for a variety of jobs and careers. Young people are understandably concerned about what subjects to take in high school, what majors to select in college, what careers to follow in order to find their place in the world. The very multiplicity of options creates confusion and anxiety. Certainly young people ought to give these matters utmost thought. They also deserve the best available advice from parents, counselors, psychologists and other professionals as to the nature and requirements of various fields of study and employment. Aptitude tests, internships, and the like provide valuable means by which to discover one's propensities, gifts and skills. Literature on vocations is abundant. Equally important is the fact that, should an undesirable path be taken, there is always the opportunity to change careers, given the flux and dynamism of modern society. Moreover, for those of us who live in the developed world, we ought to be grateful and never forget that billions of people on this globe would feel exceedingly fortunate to have any steady job at all.

What lessons can we draw from St. Paul's perspective

about "what to be" today? The first lesson would be similar to that addressed by Bishop Gerasimos to the seminarian. St. Paul has little to say about the complexities and details of matching personal gifts and careers in the modern sense. He would raise no objections to giving proper attention to the details of life's necessities, but his concern would be not to lose sight of priorities. The primary and central call of every Christian, indeed of every human being, is "to lead a life worthy of God, who calls you into his own kingdom and glory" (1 Thess 2:12). For Paul that calling meant a summons to be a follower of Christ. In the manner of Bishop Gerasimos he could write: "Whatever you do, in word or deed, do everything in the name of the Lord Jesus, giving thanks to God the Father through him" (Col 3:17). And again, be whatever you choose according to your good judgment, and do whatever comes your way according to your heart, "only let your manner of life be worthy of the gospel of Christ" (1 Phil 1:27).

But why is it so important that a person in pursuit of a vocation should lead a life worthy of God? A second implied lesson from St. Paul's life and thought is that, whatever needs might have to be addressed in life and whatever successes might be achieved in the world, human beings cannot ultimately derive their worth, and their true fulfillment, from the things of the world. Such a mindset and pursuit inevitably leads to idolatry. The worship of the things of this world is the greatest temptation of contemporary Western society, the equivalent of a kind of new paganism. People can be successful in careers but complete failures in life. Only God in his abiding love and plentitude can satisfy the deepest longings of the human heart and provide the grace for the flowering of true humanity. For Christians, only in Christ can one attain to the fullness of authentic humanity created in the image and likeness of God.[21] For St. Paul, the goal of "what to be" is intimately related to "who to be" – to be in Christ, to be united with Christ, to have the mind of Christ, to grow in "the knowledge of the Son of God, to mature personhood, to the measure of the stature of the fullness of Christ" (Eph 4:13).

A third implied lesson from the case of Paul is that, having settled with God and seeking to lead a life worthy of God, a man or woman would function basically not out of individual judgment and self-interest, but rather from the consciousness of a theocentric and communal vision. He or she would seek to live as a transformed person, a person always striving to be God-centered, love-centered, and service-centered. That factor marks the key criterion in arriving at the proper definitions of what we mean by calling, profession, or employment. To give some examples, a supreme calling such as the priesthood, without a consistent theocentric and communal focus, would eventually become a parody of the priesthood, perhaps a case of desperate survival. A profession such as being a lawyer, without a profound sense of justice and responsibility to society, would soon distort the whole nature and purpose of the legal profession and turn it into a way of social power and personal enrichment. Any profession without a deep sense of commitment and service to others can easily become mere employment. On the other hand, any job or employment, conducted from the perspective of leading a life worthy of God, would itself be transformed into a calling, indeed an ongoing sacrament, conducted for the love of God and the service of others. In that sense, the early Christians, both in the Church and in society, although the least in status by worldly standards, were nevertheless the salt and the light of the earth because their whole life was seen and lived as a calling by God.

The Question of How to Be

St. Paul provides countless inspirational exhortations about how Christians ought live a life worthy of God according to their identity and vocation. To the Christians in Corinth he writes: "Be watchful, stand firm in your faith, be courageous, be strong. Let all that you do be done in love" (1 Cor 16:13). To the Christians in Rome he exhorts: "Let love be genuine; hate what is evil, hold fast to what is good; love one another with brotherly affection; outdo one another in showing honor. Never flag in zeal, be aglow with the Spirit, serve the Lord" (Rom 12:9-11). With respect to society, he tells the Thessalonian Christians: "Aspire to live quietly, to mind your own affairs, and to work with your hands, as we charged you; so that you may command the respect of outsiders, and be dependent on nobody" (1 Thess 4:11-12). Again to the Roman Christians regarding outsiders:

> Bless those who persecute you; bless and do not curse them; rejoice with those who rejoice, weep with those who weep... Repay no one evil for evil, but take thought for what is noble in the sight of all. If possible, so far as it depends upon you, live peaceably with all... Do not be overcome by evil, but overcome evil with good. (Rom 12:14, 17-18, 21)

Not in a few places, just as any Hellenistic moralist, St. Paul gives general exhortations of universal import and beauty:

> Whatever is true, whatever is honorable, whatever is just, whatever is pure, whatever is lovely, whatever is gracious, if there is any excellence, if there is anything worthy of praise, think about these things. (Phil 4:8)

In one particular place, while exhorting Christians, he sums up his own vision of how to live a life worthy of God, which he invites Christians to follow:

> So, whether you eat or drink, or whatever you do, do all to the glory of God. Give no offense to Jews or to Greeks or to the Church of God, just as I try to please all people in everything that I do, not seeking my own advantage, but that of many, that they may be saved. Be imitators of me, as I am of Christ. (1 Cor 10:31-11:1)

The preceding counsel sounds general but the references to the glory of God and to Christ, together with the expressed concern for the salvation of all people, remind us of what we have called Paul's theocentric and communal orientation. Here we find the Apostle's deepest presuppositions, forming a vision that embraces all people for the purpose of discovering and living the true humanity in Christ and all for the glory of God. Such a vision, as already stated, is grounded in God's action, God's new world, God's new way of living, starting with the early Christians and intended for all God's people. The goal is that they all may enjoy God's blessings without compulsion or discrimination, enacting in their own personal existence the reality of a life worthy of God. For Paul, by God's action and grace, this is nothing less that a matter of radical transformation toward a new human identity in Christ – literally putting off the old nature and putting on the new nature, "which is being renewed in knowledge after the image of the Creator. Here there cannot be Greek and Jew, circumcised and uncircumcised, barbarian, Scythian, slave, free man, but Christ is all, and in all" (Col 3:10-11). A similar statement of revolutionary import, including unprecedented equality in the dignity of genders, occurs in Galatians 3:27-28: "For as many of you as were baptized into Christ have put on Christ. There is neither Jew nor Greek, there is neither slave nor free, there is neither male or female; for you are all one in Christ Jesus."

If that is the core of the Apostle's thought, is there a way to organize his diverse statements about "how to be" in the world by which to integrate his theology and ethics, and at the same time show by more specific categories how to live out our calling as Christians? We may just have such a structural paradigm in St. Paul's famous trilogy of faith, hope and love. These three words occur close together in several passages and represent far more than a rhetorical flourish (Rom 5:1-5; 1 Cor 13:13; 1 Thess 1:3).[22] Brief reflections on how faith, hope and love express the basic categories of living a life worthy of God will conclude this paper. While our exposition assumes a Christian perspective, the trilogy of faith, hope and love certainly has useful universal applications.

It is axiomatic for St. Paul that humanity is justified before God by faith. "The righteousness of God is revealed [in the gospel] from faith to faith as it is written, 'He who is righteous will live through faith'" (Rom 1:17). Faith may be defined as trust, fidelity, loyalty, commitment, and the like, especially pertaining to God. But faith for the Apostle is not general faith, a kind of positive disposition of trust in the goodness and good outcome of all things, although this is not an unhelpful thing in itself. Rather faith is faith specifically in the God of Israel, the true God and Creator of all things, and faith in Jesus the Christ through whom God has inaugurated his new world and his new way of living for all humanity. Paul's whole argument in the early chapters of Romans, where he exposes humanity's universal sinfulness and degradation (Rom 3:1:18-3:20), pivots around the good news that God's righteousness has now become manifest and effective for all through faith in Christ and the redemption in him (Rom 3:21-26). It is this kind of specific faith that St. Paul refers when he sums up his argument in Romans 5:1: "Therefore, since we are justified by faith, we have peace with God through our Lord Jesus Christ." The Apostle can invoke faith even in practical matters of what to eat or not to eat, and what special days to observe or not to observe, but always in reference to Christ and in thankfulness to God the Father (Rom 14:1-9). In Paul's letters, faith has a theocentric and christocentric orientation. It is in this sense of faith's orientation to God and to Christ that Christians are admonished always to "act from faith; for whatever does not proceed from faith is sin" (Rom 14:23).

The Greek word for faith (*pistis*), following the Hebrew nuance behind it, means not only trust but also fidelity, that is, faithfulness. Paul speaks of God's faithfulness (*pistis Theou*, Rom 3:3)[23] and of God being faithful (*pistos*).[24] God is faithful in that he is utterly reliable, true to his covenant promises, unfailingly trustworthy in his word, and now trustworthy in the good news about the new creation and the new humanity he freely offers to all in Christ. However, just as God is faithful, so also believers ought to be characterized by faithfulness to God, that is, to be trustworthy, loyal, and obedient to God, the exemplary model being Abraham in his unwavering faithfulness to God (Rom 4). The first task of faithful obedience to God is to receive the good news about Christ, and thus to enter into God's new age, to be transformed in heart and mind, and to propel the immense wave of God's grace forward by one's concrete witness. What saves is not exactly faith as a mere human capacity but as an obedient response and commitment to the gospel. Faith is a necessary response, but what alone saves is God's power and God's free gift to be attested by evidence of the new life that God grants in the believer's concrete course of life. Thus we have the superb proclamation in Ephesians 2:8-20:

> For by grace you have been saved through faith; and this is not your own doing, it is the gift of God – not because of works, lest any man should boast. For we are his workmanship, created in Christ Jesus for good works, which God prepared beforehand, that we should walk in them.

Hope is closely related both to faith and to love, the latter two being the anchors of hope. For St. Paul, once again, hope does not express a kind of undefined optimism about the future, although this is not a bad thing either. Rather Christian hope is filled with content since it is founded on what God has already done and what God will do in the future. Christian hope is unshakable, just as Christian faith and love are unshakable, because all three are dependent on God and his new order of life set forth in Christ and the Spirit. To say that we are justified by faith is to say that "we have obtained access through Christ in the grace in which we stand, and [thus] we rejoice[25] in our hope (*ep' elpidi*) of [sharing] the glory of God" (Rom 5:2). In other words, the basis of our hope is God's accomplished action in Christ. God's glory is God's holy presence, his divine radiance, his power and majesty now active in Christ. Sharing in God's glory – true communion and life with God – is what sinful humanity had lost and now can freely begin to recover in Christ (Rom 3:23-24). To come to the heart of the matter, the Apostle states that Christ himself, the mystery of the risen and living Christ in us, is our hope of glory (Col 1:27).[26]

God is the "God of hope." St. Paul prays for the Roman Christians: "May the God of hope fill you with all joy and peace in believing, so that by the power of the Holy Spirit you may abound in hope" (Rom 15:13). God is the God of hope because he is true and faithful. For exactly the same reason he is the "God of all comfort, who comforts us in all our affliction" (2 Cor 1:3-4). When Paul suffered nearly unto death in Ephesus, he set his hope on God's deliverance, relying "not on ourselves but on God who raises the dead" (2 Cor 1:8-10; 1 Cor 15:32). Faith in God's character and faithfulness, testified by God's present blessings in Christ, is what sustains Christian hope in the present life of trials and afflictions.

For Paul, the present course is a life of hope. Just as we have been justified by faith, so also "we have been saved by hope" (Rom 8:24). The fullness of glory lies ahead in God's future. For now we share in the sufferings of Christ in the hope that we shall share in his glory. St. Paul has no illusions about the destructive work of evil forces in the world that Christians must battle daily. He offers no promises about a life of ease, walking along a path of roses. In Romans 8:18-27, the Apostle makes clear that for the present time we "groan in travail" along with all creation because the marks of corruption and death are on all things. However, the new life in Christ is an invincible gift, provided that Christians remain faithful to their calling. For Paul the present sufferings are nothing as compared to the coming glory in which creation itself will be freed from the corruptive powers. We now groan for the fullness of redemption precisely because we already have tasted the first fruits of the new creation. Our hope rests above all in the gift of "Christ in you" and the indwelling Spirit in whom we cry "Abba, Father." (Rom 8:10,15). The active presence of the Spirit, God's power, intercedes for us, and gives the assurance of hope deep within us:

> It is the Spirit himself bearing witness with our spirit that we are children of God, and if children, then heirs, heirs of God and fellow heirs with Christ, provided we suffer with him in order that we may also be glorified with him. (Rom 8:16-17)

The summit of faith and hope is love. St. Paul makes countless references to love and how Christians owe nothing to anyone but to love, abound in love for each other and for all, walk in love, speak the truth in love, serve in love, be rooted and grounded in love, and do all things in love.[27] The Christians themselves are designated as those "who love God" and who are the "beloved of God and of the Lord."[28] Paul's appeals to love and his use of the language of love are so extensive as to make every thinking person pause and reflect. This phenomenon points to the core experience of the early Christians, the experience of the new creation, and the consequent astonishing development of the language of love unprecedented in the ancient world. Although closely linked to both faith and hope, love is the higher gift. St. Paul writes: "So faith, hope, love abide, these three; but the greatest of these is love" (1 Cor 3:13).

Why is love the higher gift? Why does St. Paul list love as the first gift of the Spirit ("But the fruit of the Spirit is love, joy, peace," etc.)? For the Apostle, it must again be said, love is not a general sentiment of warm affection toward others, although such sentiments are surely welcome. Love, just as much as faith and hope, bears theocentric and communal meaning within God's new order of existence testified by Christians as they live in community and seek to share the treasure of love with all. In 1 Cor 13:1-13, known as Paul's famous poem on love,[29] two reasons may be discerned. One is that love, by its selfless and patient nature, provides the key to the harmonious use of all the gifts with which Christians and all people are endowed that they may live in harmony and concord. The other is that, while the gifts such as knowledge, prophecy, faith, and hope are temporary and necessary in the present course of life, love abides forever. Even now, "love bears all things, believes all things, hopes all things, endures all things" (1 Cor 13:7).[30] But this is not a mere rhetorical statement meaning that love is mindless, ever credulous, and Pollyannaish.[31] Rather it is a statement about a love that derives from God's love in Christ, a love that is full of patience and faith, full of hope and endurance, because of what God has already accomplished and what he will accomplish in the future through eternal life in love.

Love is also preeminent for Paul because love is the fulfillment of the law of Moses, the heart of Paul's religious heritage. Jesus had spoken about the centrality of love and how love of God and love of neighbor are the greatest commandments, fulfilling the law and the prophets.[32] St. Paul who claimed to have the "mind of Christ" (1 Cor 2:16) was of the same view. In Galatians 5:13-14 he counsels responsible freedom from the Mosaic law through the practice of love insofar as the whole law of Moses is fulfilled by God's specific commandment to love one's neighbor as oneself (Gal 5:14; Lev 19:18). In Christ, Paul says, what counts is "neither circumcision nor uncircumcision…, but faith working through love" (Gal 5:6). In Romans 13:8-10 the Apostle explicitly refers to the Decalogue commandments concerning adultery, murder, theft, and covetousness. Any such thing is unthinkable for one who loves others in God and in Christ. His point is that Christians are indebted to keep but one law, the law of love which fulfills all the commandments of the law of Moses. The law of love, according to Paul, is the basis of mutual edification in the community, of bearing each other's burdens, of serving one another in love, of building up the whole community and society in love – that is the way of Christ, the very "law of Christ" (Gal 6:2; Rom 15:1-3).[33]

The most important reason for the preeminence of love, according to the Apostle, is that love derives from God himself – it is God's love for the whole world and for each person in it. For Paul the greatness of God's love is testified by the fact that, while we were ungodly and sinners, while humanity was utterly lost in idolatry, wickedness, and depravity, Christ died for us reconciling us to God (Rom 1:18-3:20; 5:6-10; Eph 2:4-7). The palpable testimony of God's love, which is also the invincible source of hope in spite of suffering, is that God's love has already been poured out in the hearts of believers. Echoing the sentiments of Jesus about rejoicing when persecuted (Matt 5:11-12), Paul can exhort

the Roman Christians to boast and celebrate in afflictions, which strengthen endurance and hope, precisely
because of the greater power of the experience of God's
love:

> We rejoice[34] in our sufferings, knowing that suffer-
> ing produces endurance, and endurance produces
> character, and character produces hope, and hope
> does not disappoint us, because God's love has been
> poured into our hearts through the Holy Spirit which
> has been given to us. (Rom 5:3-5)

The zenith of St. Paul's celebration of God's love is
not in 1 Corinthians 13 but Romans 8:28-39. Here most
clearly faith, hope, and love are centered on the greatness of God's love with which he loved humanity, "he
who did not spare his own Son but gave him up for us
all" (Rom 8:32). When the Apostle wrote his famous
words that "all things work for good for those who
love God," he meant specifically that *God himself works
all things for good with those who love him and who are
called according to his purpose* (Rom 8:28). The context of
the passage luminously speaks of God's call and God's
eternal plan to shape all humanity in conformity with
"the image of his Son" (Rom 8:28-30).[35] For Paul the
process of God's new creation has already gloriously
begun by the gift of God's Son and God's Spirit, the basis of the ongoing transformation of humanity as well
as eventually of the cosmos (Rom 8:1-30). And now the
Apostle breaks into a veritable explosion of confidence
and celebration about what a life worthy of God and
of Christ means in depth and breadth. He asks trium-
phantly: "If God is for us, who is against us?... Who
shall bring any charge against God's elect?... Who
shall separate us from the love of Christ? Shall tribula-

tion, or distress, or persecution, or famine, or nakedness, or peril, or sword?"[36] And the Apostle concludes
with these immortal words:

> No, in all these things we are more than conquerors
> through him who loved us. For I am sure that neither
> death, nor life, nor angels, no principalities, nor things
> present, nor things to come, nor powers, nor height,
> nor depth, nor anything else in all creation, will be
> able to separate us from the love of God in Christ
> Jesus our Lord. (Rom 8:37-39)

Notes

1 I owe this insight to Francis Kelly Nemeck and Marie Theresa
Coombs, *Called by God: A Theology of Vocation and Lifelong Commit-
ment* (Collegeville, MN: The Liturgical Press, 1992), 2-4. However,
I develop this paradigm in my own way with reference to St. Paul
and to the contemporary situation as I see it.
2 See for example, Paul C. Vitz, *Psychology as Religion: the Cult of
Self-Worship* (Grand Rapids: Eerdmans Publishing, 1977); Stanley
J. Grenz, *A Primer on Postmodernism* (Grand Rapids: Eerdmans
Publishing, 1996), and Peter Kreeft, *How to Win the Culture War*
(Downers Grove: InterVarsity, 2002).
3 This is not to say that there are not seekers after the deeper questions about God and abiding moral and spiritual values. For example, see Colleen Carroll, *The New Faithful: Why Young Adults Are
Embracing Christian Orthodoxy* (Chicago: Loyola Press, 2002), who
explores the lives of many young Catholics who hunger spiritually and find fulfillment in traditional Christianity with emphasis
on personal faith and authenticity.
4 This may be a rather harsh judgment but it must be said because
the influence of secular values has an impact on all of us one way
or another. Dennis M. Campbell, *Who Will Go for Us: An Invitation
to Ordained Ministry* (Nashville: Abingdon, 1994), 11-12, points
out that most people today choose a career not in terms of commitment and service but in terms of the opportunity to acquire
positions with high pay, security and "no risk." Even colleges and

universities promote this outlook in their promotional literature, priding themselves on their successes in placing students in prime positions or graduate programs promising lucrative careers.

5 See especially Galatians 1:13-14 and Philippians 3:5-6.

6 These words may be translated in various ways but the overall point is about monotheism, a confession of faith in the only true God, the living God of Abraham, Isaac and Jacob.

7 More on this universal vision rooted in Israelite history and community, see Walter Brueggemann, *An Introduction to the Old Testament: The Canon and Christian Imagination* (Louisville: Westminster John Knox Press, 2003, especially 159-75.

8 For the complex dynamics of Jewish society in the days of St. Paul, see among others James C. VanderKam, *An Introduction to Early Judaism* (Grand Rapids: Eerdmans Publishing Co., 2001), Anthony J. Saldarini, *Pharisees, Scribes and Sadducees in Palestinian Society* (Grand Rapids: Eerdmans Publishing Co., 2001), and Calvin J. Roetzel, *The World That Shaped the New Testament* (Louisville: Westminster John Knox Press, 2002).

9 On the Damascus experience and its consequences, see the various perspectives by James D. G. Dunn, *The Theology of Paul the Apostle* (Grand Rapids: Eerdmans Publishing Co., 1998), 346-54; Martin Hengel and Anna Maria Schwemer, *Paul: Between Damascus and Antioch, the Unknown Years,* trans. John Bowden (Louisville: Westminster John Knox Press, 1997), 25, 91-98, 36-43; Krister Stendahl, *Paul Among Jews and Gentiles* (Philadelphia: Fortress Press, 1976), 7-23, 78-96; Alan F. Segal, *Paul the Convert: The Apostolate and Apostasy of Saul the Pharisee* (New Haven: Yale University Press, 1990), and H. J. Schoeps, *Paul: The Theology of the Apostle in the Light of Jewish Religious History,* trans. Harold Knight (Philadelphia: Westminster Press, 1961), 54-55.

10 The only personal sin he mentions is that of persecuting the Church which he calls the Church of God (1 Cor 15:9).

11 Echoing the teaching of Jesus, the former fanatic could now write as a Christian: "Bless those who persecute you; bless and do not curse them. Rejoice with those who rejoice, weep with those who weep… Repay no one evil for evil, but take thought for what is noble in the sight of all. If possible, so far as it depends upon you, live peaceably with all… Do not be overcome by evil, but overcome evil with good" (Rom 12:4-21).

12 Constructive critique of the life of the Church is intrinsic to Orthodox teaching based on the concept of the "conscience of the Church" (*syneidesis tes ekklesias*) as a whole, which makes each Orthodox Christian responsible and accountable for the state of the Church before God.

13 To gain Roman citizenship, it may be that an ancestor had been a beloved slave who was eventually freed and adopted by his Roman master or that he had rendered some great service to Rome and thus obtained the coveted prize. For an overview of St. Paul's life and thought, see Joseph A. Fitzmeyer, *Paul and His Theology: A Brief Sketch* (Englewood Cliffs: Prentice Hall, 1987).

14 The Book of Acts refers to Paul as Saul even after his conversion.

15 It should be noted that he had no authority whatever over Gentile Christians, few as these may have been in the earliest years of the new movement.

16 Jesus had instructed that those who preached the gospel deserved to live by the gospel. See 1 Cor 9:14, 18; Luke 10:7; Matt 10:10.

17 He names many of them, among them Barnabas, Silas, Timothy, Mark, Titus and others.

18 In 1 Tim 2:4 we read that God "desires all people to be saved and to come to the knowledge of the truth."

19 He writes in 1 Cor 5:9: "I wrote to you in my letter not to associate with immoral men; not at all meaning the immoral of this world, or the greedy and robbers, or idolaters, since then you would need to go out of the world." And again in Phil 2:14-16: "Do all things without grumbling or questioning, that you may be blameless and innocent, children of God without blemish in the midst of a crooked and perverse generation, among whom you shine as lights in the world, holding fast the word of life."

20 Scholars debate the meaning of 1 Cor 7:21, whether or not Christian slaves were to avail themselves of the opportunity of freedom. In my view, the context and specific phraseology (*all' ei kai*, "and even if") favors the option of remaining a slave, or at least that the matter was of secondary importance. Paul's conclusion is clear: "So, brethren, in whatever state each was called, there let him remain with God" (1 Cor 7:24). It must also be said, however, that Christians masters were admonished to treat their

slaves as brothers in Christ (Phlm 16).

21 An insightful piece on this topic from a contemporary perspective is by Stanley J. Grenz, "The Social Imago: The Image of God and the Postmodern (Loss of) Self" in *The Papers of the Henry Luce III Fellows in Theology*, vol. VI, ed. Christopher I. Wilkins (Pittsburgh: Association of Theological Schools, 2003), 49-78.

22 It may be instructive for the reader at this point to open to Rom 5:1-5, read the text two or three times, and keep it open for the remainder of our discussion.

23 And in parallel perhaps the faith of Christ (*pistis Christou*, Rom 3:22) in the sense of the faithfulness and obedience of Jesus to the task of redemption assigned to him by the Father.

24 1 Cor 1:9; 10:13; 2 Cor 1:18; 1 Thess 5:24.

25 The Greek verb literally means to "boast" but in the sense of rejoicing and celebrating.

26 It is worth quoting here Colossians 1:27-28: "To them God chose to make known how great armong the Gentiles are the riches of the glory of this mystery, which is Christ in you, the hope of glory. Him we proclaim, warning every person and teaching every person in all wisdom, that we may present every person mature in Christ.

27 For example, Rom 8:28; 13:8; 1 Cor 16:13; Gal 5:13; Eph 3:17; 4:2; 5:2; 6:24; 1 Thess 3:12.

28 For example, Rom 1:1; Col 3:12; 1 Thess 1:4; 2 Thess 2:13.

29 The passage is superbly lyrical, but technically it is not actually a poem.

30 The meaning of "believes all things" and "hopes all things" properly understood is not that love is superficial and credulous but rather that love is filled with faith and hope in all circumstances.

31 Pollyannaish, according to Webster's, is "one who is characterized by an irrepressible optimism and the tendency to find good in everything." St. Paul was far too aware of fallen human nature and the forces of evil wreaking destruction in the world to entertain such disposition.

32 Matt 22:37-40.

33 The word *nomos* in Galatians 6:2 means law in the sense of the preeminent example and way enacted by Christ especially by his obedience unto death, and not a specific collection of Jesus' teach-

ings viewed in a legalistic fashion. Paul exhibits many echoes of Jesus' teachings but makes no attempt to gather a strict collection of them as a moral code. His "ethics" are rooted in the reality of the new creation in which the Holy Spirit tangibly guides to moral action in love.

34 See footnote 24 in reference to the same verb.

35 In the context St. Paul uses the word "predestined" but this wrongly has led to ideas and systems of strict predestination. St. Paul is speaking here about God's plan that, no matter what, will be carried through, although many may fall aside by their lack of faith and free choice. In all his letters Paul assumes that God, out of his great love for the world which he created, leaves no one outside of his loving call to salvation in Christ.

36 Readers may be sure that Paul is not speaking here rhetorically because he himself, and other Christians besides, had already suffered such afflictions. See 2 Cor 1:8-10; 11:23-29; 1 Thess 2:14; 3:1-4.

Considering Vocation: The Witness of the Fathers

KHALED ANATOLIOS

Introduction

In many ways, the question of determining one's individual vocation is a particularly modern concern, at least insofar as it is not merely limited to a choice between the lay state and monastic or clerical life. Certainly, the range of choices available to persons living in contemporary Western societies was nonexistent in the social context of the early Church. Moreover, there is always a certain complexity in seeking a resolution for a situation that is embedded in one epoch from the legacy bequeathed to us by a vastly different historical situation. Indeed, we can anticipate the fundamental skepticism that can be evoked by this attempt in the minds of many. We can look to "the Fathers" for pious words, correct doctrine, and perspicacious insights into the "spiritual life," but can these figures of hallowed memory really have something concrete to say to me – something that could serve as the principle of concrete action – as I try to forge my way into the life of the twenty-first century?

This is a question that should not be answered precipitately and by mere pious reflex. It can be answered with integrity only if we first take stock of our own situation, the situation embedded in our own posing of the question, and then attempt to see whether there are certain perspectives available to us from the patristic tradition that can illumine our understanding of our own situation, and improve our capacity to act wisely and meaningfully within it. In the following remarks, I do not claim to give *the* patristic answer to the question of the discernment of vocation in our time. I simply offer one attempt to bring our own situation into conversation with the witness of the fathers and mothers of the early Church with regard to this vital question.

Discerning the Signs of Our Times

Let us begin then by analyzing the situation driving contemporary Christians to ask this question of vocation. What are the presuppositions, aspirations, and hidden questions involved in the explicit posing of this question? There is a combination of influences at play, some arising directly from Christian theological and spiritual traditions and some issuing from other historical streams. It is our identification with the Judeo-Christian tradition that gives us a lively sense that a human life finds its true value and meaning when it is governed by the gift of a divine "call" and thereby dedicated and radically blessed by God. From this perspective, we can look to the figure of Abraham, who became a blessing for the whole world by allowing his life to be at the disposal of the divine calling – to be at God's "beck and call."[1] But the figure of Abraham, while being paradigmatic in a symbolic sense, also evokes a sense of the distinctiveness of our own situation. Abraham was led by God through long wanderings in order to found a "promised land" to be populated by God's chosen people, the Israelites. But we find ourselves in a world that often seems oblivious and inhospitable to Christian or even theistic concerns, a world that seems to be radically resistant to becoming a "promised land." The question of vocation forces us to ask how we could negotiate our way in the midst of this world in a manner that is still enfolded by a divine calling. Raising this question also imposes on us certain ideological and psychological pressures that emanate from the *Zeitgeist* of our contemporary Western culture. In this culture, the question of vocation construed simply as that of deciding what to do with one's life – and quite concretely as that of choosing a profession – is considered with reference to the value of "self-fulfillment."

To some extent, the category of "self-fulfillment" merely restates in a modern idiom the notion of happiness, and no one would deny that this is something for which it is both natural and good to strive. There is, however, a peculiarly modern problematic lurking around the category of self-fulfillment which raises the question of vocation from a practical problem to be faced at one stage of one's life to an existential dilemma that pervades modern existence. The problem is that, while the modern ethos champions self-fulfillment as an absolute value, it is decidedly ambivalent about what constitutes the self and what constitutes fulfillment. At the heart of this ambivalence, in turn, is a radical ambivalence about the inherent meaning of reality itself, considered as a whole. In classical terms, the happiness of the self depended on its harmonization with the inherent order, meaning, and goal (*telos*) of reality. But in a worldview in which there is actually no world of order and meaning, the self cannot achieve any happiness of harmonizing itself within a whole, has no way of making itself "at home."[2] Within such an understanding, self-fulfillment can only be conceived as blank self-assertion. Self-fulfillment means a perpetual self-creation out of nothing and then the assertion of this self-creation against all obstacles. This is a short summary of Nietzsche's notion of "will to power" – self-fulfillment as blank self-assertion – but many of our contemporaries who have never heard of Nietzsche conceive of their life task in basically these terms.[3]

The vocabulary of Hollywood piety is replete with subliminal references to this worldview of self-creation and self-assertion: "Follow your passions"; "Believe in yourself"; "Don't let anything stand in your way." Of course, none of these slogans are malicious in themselves; the concern rather is in what they leave out. Life here is simply a transaction between the self and its own powers of assertion. Ultimately, there can be no sense of vocation here, no call addressed to the self from outside of it, no response that the self is solicited to make to an other, no home for the self to inhabit. In many ways, this sense of radical existential homelessness is the pervasive milieu of modern existence. The strategies of coping with it are various. Some currents of modern culture invite us to merely enjoy the "play" of our tenuous efforts at self-construction, without presuming to hope for any stable relationship with an inherently meaningful reality.[4] Most of us more or less unthinkingly adopt a plebian version of such a strategy undergirded by the fundamental agenda of the "will to power." We cultivate "passions" because these represent experiences of the intensification of the self and we try to satisfy these passions, while drifting lightly from one series of experiences to another without presuming to settle into any stable or covenantal pattern of interacting with reality.

The Patristic Witness: Vocation
and the Christian Narrative

If the above description represents accurately at least some elements of our modern experience, it should lead us to make distinctive demands of our inquiry into the "mind of the Fathers." We cannot be looking merely for some pious words about how good and necessary it is "to serve God and neighbor." We must internalize the full impact of how the worldview of the fathers and mothers of Christian tradition collides with the currents of our modern world-view. In the worldview of Christian tradition, the self is not radically homeless but finds its home in a universe inherently designed to lead humanity to rejoice in the beautiful intelligibility of a loving God. The human person is ordained to find her fulfillment by cooperating with this divine plan to bring all things to union with him and in him. Ultimately, the human self finds its home by immersing itself in the *economia* (or history of salvific interaction) through which God himself makes his home within human reality, thereby enabling humanity to make its home in the domain of divine life. Such a worldview soberly notes all the ways in which this radical human vocation is derailed by human sinfulness but then joyfully proclaims that this derailment is always amenable to healing through God's salvific work in Christ.

All the spiritual and intellectual exertions of the patristic tradition referred to this core Christian narrative in which humanity as a whole had a divinely-ordained vocation within a meaningful universe whose ultimate goal was the eternal delight of union with God. A properly Christian view of the question of vocation must commence from this core narrative, centered on the economy of the humanization of God and the deification of humanity. Nevertheless, once we acknowledge the centrality of this account as answering the question of human vocation in the most radical and universal terms, we can then ask whether we can interpret this core narrative with a particular application to the practical question of wondering quite simply what to do with one's life. I would like to propose that one such exegesis could be constructed by applying a model of Christian life, articulated in both Eastern and Western patristic and medieval traditions, in terms of the stages of purification, illumination, and union.[5] In applying this model, we are not leaving behind the core Christian narrative of the *economia* that culminates in divine humanization and human deification but simply applying it concretely and specifically to the question of vocation.

Discerning Vocation: The Dimension of Purification

We have already mentioned the tendency in our contemporary Western culture to view self-fulfillment as dedication to whatever happens to be one's current desires: "Follow your passion." The problem once again of course is that this approach abstracts from any sense of objective standards by which one's "passions" are evaluated. Taken literally, the commandment to "follow your passion" can be fulfilled equally by a saint and a serial killer. The implicit ethos is one that seeks a value-free assertion of the self, rather than providing guidance for the formation of the self. The Christian tradition, however, provides a different perspective. The core narrative of Christian faith, which both affirms humanity's vocation to communion with God as well as human beings' tendency to betray this vocation, leads to a sense of critical realism in the evaluation of one's "passions." Already in the fourth century, Athanasius provides us with a critique of what sounds much like the postmodern tendency to exult in the mere assertion of the self apart from consideration of the moral value of the goal of such exertion. He sees this value-less indulgence in the sheer motion of the soul as fundamental to the dynamism of sin:

> The body has eyes in order to see creation and to recognize the Creator through this harmonious order, and it has hearing in order to listen to the divine sayings and the laws of God, and it has hands in order to accomplish necessary actions and in order to extend them toward God in prayer. But when the soul turned away from contemplation of the good and from movement within the good, it was henceforth deceived and moved toward the opposite. Then, having in view its own power, as we said before, and abusing it, it realized that it can also move its bodily members in the opposite direction. So instead of looking at creation, it turned its eyes toward desires, showing that it can do that too. It thought that as long as it was in motion it would preserve its own dignity and would not be in error in actualizing its capabilities. It did not realize that it was brought into being not merely to be in motion but to move toward what it should. Therefore, the apostolic saying commands, "All things are possible but not all are expedient." (1 Cor 6:12) But human presumption, not regarding what is appropriate and fitting but only its

own power, began to do the opposite.[6]

St. Athanasius presents us here with both an affirmation of the theocentric vocation of humanity and all creation and a critique of the notion of human self-fulfillment conceived as the will to power. The Christian realism of the fathers and mothers of the early Church contained a deep understanding that this critique of "self-fulfillment" was not merely an intellectual observation but a daily struggle for the Christian. Hence, we have the ascetical understanding of Christian life, which, especially in our Eastern tradition, is understood not merely as one option among many possibilities of "Christian lifestyles," but as simply an intrinsic and ineradicable feature of Christian existence.[7]

Indeed, this conception of Christian existence as one of struggle against our pervasive tendencies to betray our Godward vocation is prominent in the Christian rite of baptism. In the rite of baptism, we are made aware that a life in communion with God entails the rejection of "Satan and all his pomp." The Fathers were very concerned that the circumstances of one's life and work must be evaluated by and harmonized with the standards of Christian baptism. For example, St. Gregory of Nyssa declares forthrightly that a person who does not revise the concrete circumstances of his life in keeping with the likeness of God – a likeness sacramentally offered to him through baptism – obtains no benefit from the sacrament:

> Those who are wronged, defrauded, and deprived of their property observe, for their part, no change when a man like this is baptized. They do not hear him saying what Zacchaeus said: "If I have defrauded anyone of anything, I will restore him fourfold." What they said

of him before baptism, they continue to say of him now. They call him by the same names – a covetous person, greedy for others' property, and feeding on men's misfortunes. A man then who remains the same and yet prattles to himself about the change for the better he has undergone in baptism, should attend to what Paul says: "If anyone thinks he is something when he is nothing, he deceives himself." For you are not what you have not become; whereas the gospel says of the regenerate that 'He gave all those who received him the power to become God's children.' Now the child born of someone certainly shares his parent's nature. If, then, you have received God and become his child, let your way of life testify to the God within you; make it clear who your Father is![8]

In this excerpt from St. Gregory of Nyssa, we find an example of the coherence and wholeness of the Patristic vision wherein the ontological vocation of the human being to be "God's image", the sacramental life of the Church, and the concrete circumstances of one's daily life are seen to be all of a piece. Such a perspective can offer a radical challenge to a tendency to see the exigency of "making a good living" as something separable from the "spiritual" life of faith. If we try to apply such a consistent vision to the concrete situation of a contemporary Christian seeking to discern her vocation, what can we say?

First, approaching the question of discerning one's vocation must begin with a prayerful evaluation of one's guiding motivations. The first question then becomes whether our motivations are consistent with the radical human vocation to participate in and contribute to creation's communion with God or are manifestations of distorted passions: greed for material wealth, desire for self-aggrandizement, lust for power over others, etc.

At this stage, the dimension of purification is applied
to our subjective approach to the question of our vocation. It needs to be said, perhaps, that such a purification is not merely a matter of weeding out desires that
in themselves tend to evil or malicious actions. The patristic approach to Christian ethics is never so simply
legalistic as to merely divide what is allowable from
what is not allowable. Rather, it is an approach that
seeks to anchor ethical life in the ultimate hope of deification.[9] From such a perspective, the "purification" of
one's motivations preparatory to a discernment of vocation must include the positive trajectory of a desire
to be entirely and whole-heartedly at the disposal of
God. Concretely, this will sometimes mean the subor-
dination of not only peer but also familial pressures in
the process of discernment. Beginning with Jesus himself, the Christian tradition is replete with examples
that dramatize the necessity of prioritizing one's fidelity to a divine will and call over any competing social
pressures (cf. Luke 2:41-52; Luke 8:19-21).

Ultimately, then, the movement of purification in the
discernment of one's vocation follows a trajectory that
is oriented toward the union of one's human will with
the divine will. The time of choosing one's vocation is
a privileged occasion to exercise a fundamental option
toward this union of wills. Consequently, it is at the
same time an opportunity to enter into the christological drama of salvation. St. Maximos the Confessor has
depicted this drama of salvation with special reference
to the mystery of the union of divine and human wills
in Christ. At the cost of torture and the cutting off of
his tongue, St. Maximos insisted that the mystery of
our salvation is accomplished through Christ's posses-
sion of an integral human will which he subjected to

the divine will, thereby modeling in himself the union in freedom between humanity and God.[10] All this was not abstract speculation for Maximos but concrete and urgent enough for him to suffer physical torture. The time of discerning one's vocation is an equally serious occasion for any Christian to give witness (*martyria*) to the mystery of participation in the christological union of divine and human wills.

But the application of the category of purification to the discernment of vocation has to do not only with an evaluation of the disposition of the person making this discernment. It also has an equally significant reference to the objective import of the options under consideration. As is implied by the quotation above from St. Gregory of Nyssa, one has to consider whether these options entail a course of action that is contrary to the ethos of Christian life. With a view to this question, there needs to be a contemporary appropriation of the patristic model: today we should apply the ascetical imperative of Christian life to a social critique. There are economic and social networks in our society that are given over to the service of unjust power, gluttony, and other vices. Each vice has its own economy and the collusion of these various economies form a large part of our Western super-economies of domination and overconsumption that are gobbling up the world's resources in a wastefully disproportionate manner. The question of vocation invites us to deconstruct the artificial separation between "spiritual devotion" and interaction with the world. What sense would it make to observe faithfully the Orthodox discipline of Lent while working in an advertising agency in which I am asked to devote all my intelligence and ingenuity to entice people to indulgent consumption of things they do not really need, by means that appeal directly to their inordinate desires? The point is not finally to withdraw from the world altogether but to ask serious questions about how the actual work I do will be consistent with the Christian vision of reality. Yet there is also a positive dimension to this objective application of the category of "purification." There are indeed a great many options for work that are intrinsically oriented toward the "purification" of the world. A therapist who is dedicated to healing people from the disordered passions of addiction, an economist who works to bring about a more just distribution of wealth, a lawyer who strives to ensure that the weak are not exploited by the powerful are all involved in the work of the purification of humanity.

In sum, then, we can apply the category of "purification" to the discernment of vocation in two ways, subjectively and objectively. Subjectively, we can try to invoke prayerfully God's grace, so that our own motives in choosing a mode of life and work may be purified. Objectively, we can ask whether the options to which we are drawn undermine or contribute to the purification of all of humanity.

Discerning Vocation:
The Dimension of Illumination

If purification is considered to be the first movement of progress in Christian life, according to one classic framework, this should by no means be understood as implying a radically negative view of the world. Rather, it is the realization embedded within the Christian narrative that in the present condition of things, the true and radical goodness of creation and humanity cannot be properly appropriated without moral and spiritual exertion. The early Christian tradition expressly rejected the Manichean view that creation and material reality are radically evil. Indeed, not only the goodness of creation but also its capacity to be reflective of the divine in some measure were affirmed by the patristic tradition, and it is this focus which comes especially into view with the stage of "illumination."

For St. Maximos the Confessor, the ascent to knowledge of God begins with the "natural contemplation (*theōria physikē*)" of creation as reflective of divine wisdom and beauty. This symbolic likeness of creation to God is at the heart of Maximos' notion that created realities are manifestations of "ideas" (*logoi*) intended by God, whose coherence, harmony, and unity are found in the *Logos* himself, the eternal Word who became incarnate as Jesus the Christ. Likewise, for Maximos, the movement of history is governed by the providential *"logoi"* of God, the divine intentions which interact with human freedom in order to bring about God's designs for humanity. Ultimately, Maximos considers these designs to be encompassed by a grand christological movement, wherein the time up to the incarnation of the Word is characterized as the "age" of the humanization of God, while subsequent history is characterized as the age of deification.[11] If we take St. Maximos as our guide, we can understand the stage of "illumination" as a way of seeing history and creation christologically, as manifestations of the God revealed to us in Jesus Christ. As we did with the movement of "purification," we can now try to apply the category of "illumination" to the practical questions of discerning one's vocation.

Once again, we can also apply this category in a double way, in reference to the subjective disposition of the one asking the question of vocation and in reference to the objective orientations of certain options available to such a person. With regard to subjective disposition, we can say that the person who is inquiring about vocation needs to have at least a basic knowledge of the Christian narrative, not merely as an edifying set of "spiritual" beliefs but precisely as a christological rendering of reality and reading of the world and human history. This means that an adequate preparation for a proper Christian discernment of vocation must include education in the whole Christian vision of reality, which would cover not only Christian theology but various aspects of Christian humanism: art, literature, philosophy, etc. Without such an education, the best that can be hoped for is the kind of pious secularism so penetratingly unmasked by the great Orthodox theologian, Alexander Schmemann, in which there is a mutual excommunication of God and world.[12] Of course, such an education would also include a personal appropriation of practices of prayer, meditation, and contemplation, insofar as seeing the world christologically is a creative and highly personal act which cannot be learned from mere formulas and memorizations but has to be lived out through prayer in the Spirit.

With such a formation, a Christian will be able to conceive the possibility of a mode of work or profession that is objectively suited to the task of illuminating a christological vision of reality. It should be clear by now that such work is by no means restricted to the field of theological reflection, though it certainly includes that. Any art or science that seeks to illuminate the beauty and intelligibility of creation and the depths of the human spirit has at least an implicit contribution to the task of the christological illumination of reality and can be explicitly embraced by the Christian in that fashion.

Discerning Vocation: The Dimension of Unity

Within the schema that interprets the movement of Christian life according to the threefold pattern of purification, illumination, and union, the last stage delineates the consummation of the Christian's union with God. This stage is often described in mystical terms as a total immersion in divine love and as an ecstasy that transports the mind beyond its merely natural function. A stable and enduring realization of this experience is perhaps only an asymptotic goal in this life, of which we are afforded some glimpses through the witnesses of saints and mystics. Nevertheless, the orientation toward such a goal is integral to every Christian life and such an orientation is in fact foundational to the other stages of Christian experience, purification and illumination. Purification involves the disengagement from patterns of life that impede one's union with God, while illumination consists in the discernment of creation's innate references to the reality and beauty of God – which is to say, creation's innate readiness for union with God.

Once again, we can speak of how this orientation to union with God can be a practical factor in the Christian's discernment of vocation, according to both a subjective and objective aspect. Subjectively, it is simply a matter of having an explicit desire for union with God, which is the fruit of Christian prayer in all its forms. Such a disposition will predispose the Christian to pose the question of vocation directly in

terms of the possibility to facilitate union with God.
Objectively, we can look to the patristic tradition for a
vision of the structure of reality as inherently ordained
toward union with God. This vision is given explicit
and comprehensive expression again by St. Maximos
the Confessor. St. Maximos elaborates a christological
vision of reality that is based on faith in Jesus Christ as
the one who unites the extremes of God and creation in
his own person. For Maximos, Jesus Christ represents
and embodies the union, without confusion or mix-
ture, between the different aspects of created reality as
well as between creation as a whole and God. Integral
to this vision is Maximos' understanding that creation
itself is constituted by divisions that are ordained to
be enfolded by a harmonious union that nevertheless
preserves distinctions.[13]

In this context, Maximos speaks of a fivefold structural division of reality: God and creation; thought and
physical sensation; heaven and earth; paradise and the
inhabited world; and male and female. While these divisions are created by God for the sake of an ultimate
harmony that preserves their distinctions, sin estrang-
es the components of each pair from the other. Yet, the
work of Christ re-empowers the human person to be an
agent for the mediation and reunification of these divisions. Through Christ, the one who reconciles all things
in himself (cf. Eph 2:14-18), the Christian is enabled to
have a share in the work of reconciling masculine and
feminine traits in an integral humanity; of returning
this inhabited world to the condition of "paradise,"
which is to say, the condition of being governed by
virtue; of uniting heaven and earth by contemplating
the divine intentions or *"logoi"* manifested by creation;
of consequently seeing all sensible reality as reflective

of intelligible reality; and finally, of cooperating in the complete union "without distinction" of creation with God that is effected by the hypostatic union of divinity and humanity in Christ.

Now, what may we say of the professions in relation to this fivefold scheme? It would be difficult to think of any profession that could not be located somewhere within this grand scheme, though admittedly it would require the contemplative posture inculcated by the stage of "illumination" to discern just how that is so in the particular case. Essentially, however, it is not a matter of locating a given profession within one or other (they are by no means mutually exclusive) of the "fivefold mediations" outlined by Maximos but rather of assimilating the general vision of human activity as oriented toward the holistic harmony of creation in God, what in later Russian Orthodox thought came to be conceived under the notion of "*sobornost.*"[14] Any work that furthers the harmonious communion between human beings and between humanity and nature – ultimately with a view to the union of all creation with and in God – can be readily subsumed within this category. The work of a janitor, for example, from the point of view of christological "illumination" fulfills a ministry of "*sobornost*" in facilitating the conditions necessary for people to interact together in a benign environment.

Yet at the same time, while we can say that the category of "purification" is particularly applicable to professions that are concerned in one way or another with healing and moral guidance and that of "illumination" has special reference to the contemplative arts and sciences, so the category of "union" has a particularly direct reference to one realm of Christian vocation. In the latter case, this vocation is that of ministry in the Church and specifically the order of the priesthood. For the union and communion of humanity among itself, with creation, and ultimately with God is only fulfilled in the person of Jesus Christ, whose presence and work is mediated through the sacramental life of the Church. Through the ministry of unity exercised in the celebration of the sacraments, all the work of purification and illumination that Christians do becomes unified and transfigured in the personal unity of humanity and divinity in Jesus Christ. Thus, the work of the priest becomes united with all the work of the congregation in an offering that becomes integral to the deification of the world in Christ. It is in the sacramental life of the Church that all human work becomes integrated with the radical vocation of humanity to be deified and it is the particular work of the priest to celebrate and, by the grace of Christ, effect this integration: "If there are priests in the Church, if there is the priestly vocation in it, it is precisely in order to reveal to each vocation its priestly essence, to make the whole life of all men the liturgy of the kingdom, to reveal the Church as the royal priesthood of the redeemed world."[15]

Conclusion

For Eastern Christians, life in Christ is radically communal – which is to say, ecclesial – and this communion is understood as both encompassing and transcending history. For this reason, we place great emphasis on ecclesial tradition, seen precisely as the communion of the body of Christ extended throughout history and beyond, even reaching to the heavenly liturgy. Moreover, the Eastern Christian tradition places a particular emphasis on the life of the early Church and the consensus of the church fathers (*"consensus patrum"*) as providing an authoritative vision of the mystery of Christian life. It is natural, therefore, to look to the witness of the early Church for some guidance to the vital question which determines so much of each individual life, the question of vocation. In the preceding reflections, we have acknowledged the complexity of such an endeavor and suggested that it can be carried out only in the key of a creative conversation in which we are aware of the particularities of our own context and open to the task of transposing key insights from the thought of the early Church into a contemporary setting.

In light of these considerations, we noted that perhaps the predominant rubric under which the question of vocation tends to be broached in modern secular society is that of "self-fulfillment" and we tried to show how such a standard needs to be qualified and critiqued from the perspective of a world-view governed by the Christian narrative. We then endeavored to show how a traditional framework for viewing the dynamism of Christian life as a process of purification, illumination, and the union of creation in God can be applied to the question of discerning one's vocation. With regard to each of these dimensions of Christian life, we saw that it can be applied according to a subjective aspect concerned with the formation of the person making the discernment and according to an objective aspect that has to do with the actual work being considered. We have been concerned to show that, from the perspective of a patristic world-view, the question of individual vocation must be seen as enfolded within the larger framework of the Christian narrative of salvation (*economia*) in which the vocation of all creation to share in the life of God has been accomplished in the union of humanity and divinity in Christ. Every Christian man or woman is called to a prayerful and thoughtful discernment of how he or she is invited by God to share in the eventual embrace of all creation within the communion of love which is Father, Son, and Holy Spirit.

Notes

1 Gen 12-25.

2 On the history of conceptions of the self and the modern dilemma of the world-less self, see Charles Taylor, *Sources of the Self: The Making of the Modern Identity*. (Cambridge, MA: Harvard University Press, 1992)

3 For a general introduction to the work of Nietzsche, see Friedrich Nietzsche, *The Portable Nietzsche*, ed. and trans. Walter Kaufman (New York, Penguin, 1982)

4 On some of the tensions between the Christian vision and a popular postmodern perspective, see Joseph Feeney, SJ, "Can a Worldview Be Healed? Students and Postmodernism," *America* 177:15 (Nov. 15, 1997), 12-16 and, Johan van der Vloet, "Faith and the Postmodern Challenge," *Communio* 17 (1990), 132-139.

5 We find classic Eastern versions of this schema in Dionysius the Areopagite (6th c.) and St. Maximos the Confessor (7th c.). A modern application of this schema to Orthodox spirituality is found in D. Staniloae, *Orthodox Spirituality: A Practical Guide for the Faithful and a Definitive Manual for the Scholar*; trans. Archimandrite Jerome (Newville) & Otilia Kloos (South Canaan, PA: St. Tikhon's Seminary Press, 2002)

6 Athanasius, *Against the Greeks*, 4 .

7 On the application of the ascetic virtues to the lay state, see Paul Evdokimov, *Ages of the Spiritual Life*, trans. M. Plekon and A. Vinogradov (Crestwood, NY: St. Vladimir's Seminary Press, 1998).

8 St. Gregory of Nyssa, *Address on Religious Instruction* 40; ET: *Christology of the Later Fathers*, ed. E. Hardy in collaboration with C. Richardson. Library of Christian Classics (Philadelphia: West-

minster Press, 1954), 324.

9 The concept of "deification" is central especially for the Eastern Christian tradition. It reflects the understanding that the goal of Christian discipleship is to share in the very life of God. For further reading, see P. Nellas, *Deification in Christ: Orthodox Perspectives on the Nature of the Human Person* (Crestwood, NY: St. Vladimir's Seminary Press, 1987).

10 See St. Maximos the Confessor, *Opuscule* 3, 7 (English translation in Andrew Louth, *Maximos the Confessor*. Early Church Fathers (New York: Routledge: 2004), 180-198 and *Opuscule* 6. English translation in Paul Blowers & Robert Louis Wilken, *On the Cosmic Mystery of Jesus Christ: Selected Writings from St. Maximos the Confessor*, Popular Patristics Series. (Crestwood, NY: St. Vladimir's Seminary Press: 2003), 173-176.

11 St. Maximos the Confessor, *To Thalassius*, Question 22 (Blowers & Wilken, op.cit., 115-118) .

12 In recent times, A. Schmemann has strongly criticized this pseudo-piety which "makes life ultimately unredeemable and religiously meaningless." Cf. *For the Life of the World* (Crestwood, NY: St. Vladimir's Seminary Press, 2002, 18) – reprint from 1963.

13 For the following, see St. Maximos, *Ambiguum*, 41.

14 For a popular presentation of this notion, see Catherine de Hueck Doherty, *Sobornost: Eastern Unity of Mind and Heart for Western Man* (Notre Dame, IN: Ave Maria Press, 1977).

15 A. Schmemann, *For the Life of the World*, op. cit., 93.

In the Image of God:
Mystical Theology and Secular Vocations

Demetrios S. Katos

What could Orthodox Christianity, a tradition that prides itself as being mystical, possibly contribute to a discussion of vocation?[1] After all, mysticism is popularly associated with activities that transcend ordinary categories and experiences, whereas vocation is often identified with a professional occupation – and what could be more mundane than a job? Mystical theology, however, should not be identified with an exotic experience or the acquisition of esoteric knowledge. Early Christians used the words *mystery* and *mystical* simply to mean the Christian truth about reality, that is, to signify the spiritual reality that is present within the historical one.[2] The Christian understanding of *mystical* theology or *mysticism*, therefore, does not connote the existence of a mysterious, disconnected realm; instead, it is an interpretation of reality from a divine perspective. Properly understood, Christian mysticism does not separate believers from the world, rather it urges them to transfigure the world by perceiving God permeating its every dimension. Orthodox theology transfigures vocation and makes it sacred when it reveals previously unimaginable approaches to vocation by offering a vision of what we *are* and what we might *become*, the two foundational ideas of an ancient theology that is the legacy of all Christians: Orthodox, Catholic, and Protestant.

Created in the Image of God

Central to Christian mystical theology is the declaration of scripture that we are created in the image of God.[3] Genesis 1:26-27 states,

> Then God said, 'Let us make man in our image, after our likeness; and let them have dominion over the fish of the sea, and over the birds of the air, and over the cattle, and over all the earth.' So God created man in his own image, in the image of God he created him; male and female he created them.

For the sake of the present discussion it is necessary to comment briefly upon two important elements within this passage. First, God distinguished humanity from the rest of creation by creating it in his "image, after his likeness"; "man" (Hebrew, *'adam*) in this instance is a collective noun referring to all of humankind ('male and female he created them', a formula repeated in Genesis 5:2). Genesis 1 grants humanity a pre-eminence over the rest of creation by positing its creation last in a sequence of increasingly complex creative activity, but even a non-religious perspective might grant humanity a certain pride of place since it is the most biologically complex and intelligent species. This scriptural passage is significant because it makes a qualitative distinction between the human constitution and the rest of animal creation by asserting an intimate connection between God and humanity. This intimacy between God and humanity is pointed out again in Genesis 2:7, which says, "then the Lord God… breathed into his nostrils the breath of life, and the man became a living being." Human nature enjoys dependence on and intimacy with God, for its life is received directly from him.

Second, humanity was instructed to have dominion over the rest of the earth. Since God alone is believed to have true dominion over the world, it is clear that humanity's singular role within the created order mimics God's own role. Humanity is called to fulfill a divine task, and its designation for this task reaffirms the claim that there is a direct correlation, an immediate association or connection between it and God. This is clearly stated elsewhere in Scripture with the metaphor of the relationship between parent and child. For example, Moses is directed by God to tell Pharaoh, "Thus says the Lord, 'Israel is my first-born son,' and I say to you, 'Let my son go that he may serve me' (Exod 4:22)." God is the creator of all reality and has dominion over all, but only humanity has been deemed his child. Imagery of father and child commonly expressed a relationship of loyalty and dependence among ancient Near Eastern civilizations; that there is an intimate, spiritual character to this relationship is the contribution of the gospels and epistles. The Gospel of John writes,

> To all who receive him (i.e., Christ), who believed in his name, he gave power to become children of God, who were born, not of blood or of the will of the flesh or of the will of man, but of God. (John 1:12-13)

St. Paul says in his Epistle to the Romans,

> For all who are led by the Spirit of God are children of God … when we cry, "Abba! Father!" it is that very Spirit bearing witness with our spirit that we are children of God, and joint heirs with Christ. (Rom 8:13-17)

Here again is the assertion that humanity comes forth from God and has a divine potential. What that divine potential is, and how it is realized, was the subject of a profoundly spiritual discussion among the very first Christians.

Our Divine Potential

Early Christian theologians believed Genesis 1:26-27 meant that we are all called to become a divine image of our Creator.[4] Although our constitution is imperfect, it is created with the potential for spiritual growth and divine perfection. Consider the words of a second-century saint, Theophilus of Antioch, who wrote,

> God transferred him [Adam] out of the earth from which he was made into paradise, giving him an opportunity for progress so that by growing and becoming mature, and furthermore having been declared a god, he might also ascend into heaven (for man was created in an intermediate state, neither entirely mortal nor entirely immortal, but capable of either state; similarly the place paradise – as regards beauty – was created intermediate between the world and heaven), possessing immortality.[5]

Theophilus imagined Adam cultivating the soil of his heart with good works and obedience to the commandments of God, because "the expression 'to work' (Gen 2:15) implies no other task than keeping the commandment of God, lest by disobedience he destroy himself as he did through sin."[6]

We in turn are called to the same task of fulfilling our divine potential. Theophilus would insist that Adam was not the perfect being and that we should not wax nostalgic for a return to his state. True, he had an ideal purity that allowed him to receive God in the garden and speak with him face to face, but he was created in an intermediate state and was intended to grow and mature. Humanity did not lose divine life with Adam or because of him; rather, it failed ever to achieve it. This notion is central to a proper understanding of our identity and vocation because it encapsulates our true condition and destiny; stated otherwise, we ought not have too high an estimation of ourselves, neither ought we be self-deprecating, for we are not divine, neither are we evil. We were created with potential for true growth and this belief lies at the heart of the vocational search.

It might seem odd that theologians of the early Church needed to refute suggestions that a human being is *per se* divine, but this was the challenge they faced from other contemporary religious movements and schools that today are commonly called gnostic.[7] It is believed that some ancient religious teachers, such as Basilides and Valentinus, embraced both of the antipodes that we discussed a moment ago. These so-called gnostics observed the evil and suffering of this world, and concluded that the world was beyond redemption. More specifically, they witnessed human evil and suffering and in some way decided that humanity, or some aspect of it, was beyond redemption. Thus they asserted that true human identity must be a profoundly spiritual reality completely antithetical to what can be conceived, perceived, or contained in this world. Here lay true human identity and the sole hope of redemption, but it would only be revealed by escaping and disentangling itself from this world after death. One could argue that at the core of their belief system was the pessimistic notion that all human affairs and activities are hopelessly irredeemable.

Although such teachings might appear fantastic to-day, they are by no means irrelevant. They gave voice to a pessimism that continues to this day, which in turn is sustained by the natural and moral evil witnessed daily. At one time or another, have we not all cried in our consternation, "All men are liars!" (Ps 116:11) when we realized the pervasiveness of human weakness and evil? Is it not common to complain that all politicians are "the same," meaning at least self-serving, if not outrightly corrupt? Many do not vote, believing it will not make any difference, perhaps even perceiving themselves disenfranchised. Are not cities shaken to their foundations when police misconduct or criminal activity is uncovered? There are minority populations that perceive themselves as abandoned by the very institutions that were established to protect them. Do not crises of faith erupt when scandal is revealed in churches? There are disaffected believers of all denominations who have given up hope of redemption in and for this world. The so-called gnostic schools of ancient teachers like Valentinus and Basilides may no longer exist, but similarly escapist attitudes persist, even among Christians, who may abandon all hope for God's intervention in this age and seek solace only in the next and last age.

Yet at the heart of the Christian doctrine of the image of God is an unquenchable optimism that promises us that we can improve matters and make a difference in the world by bringing them into God's domain. Indeed, the Christian faith professes a profound optimism in human potential, from moral and spiritual reform in the current age, to resurrection and eternal life in the next. Many significant theologians of the early Church, among them Theophilus and others mentioned below, insisted that Adam had the potential to acquire even greater spiritual gifts and to achieve a relationship with God even closer than that of his original creation, and this was quite a claim, since Adam already possessed remarkable qualities and enjoyed a relationship that was intimate.

The lesson on vocation is clear here: a vocational quest that is founded upon the belief that we are in the image of God engenders persistence in the search for the optimal role to play in life. We should not merely yearn for what Adam enjoyed, rather we must reclaim it and surpass it. A hymn from the Orthodox matins service of Holy Monday illustrates this point by drawing a parallel between Adam and Jacob's youngest son, Joseph. "Leaving his garment behind him, Joseph fled from sin; and like the first man (i.e. Adam) before his disobedience, though naked he was not ashamed." [8] The hymn extols Joseph for possessing the same purity of heart as Adam before his transgression in Eden. Just as Adam was indifferent to his nakedness in the garden, so too Joseph was indifferent to his nakedness (not mentioned in Genesis, but suggested by the hymn) when he wrested himself away from his master's wife and left behind his cloak in her clutches. But his purity of heart was only the first step towards his glorification, which came after he endured suffering and ignominious imprisonment. So, too, Theophilus argued that Adam had greater glory in store for himself, had he not transgressed God's command. That is, even in the garden of Eden, Adam was not expected to be perfect, but to grow into perfection; he was expected to conform his life to the divine, not to possess it at the outset. Our lives, our vocational quests, are not different from his.

Time, perseverance, and maturity are required to bring our quests to fruition.

Locating the Divine Potential

Many early Christian authors have offered a variety of suggestions for the location of divine potential in humanity, including the body, intellectual faculties (e.g., reason and free will), spiritual qualities (e.g., virtue), and divine gifts (e.g., grace of adoption and sonship), but one thing underlines all of them: the necessity to sanctify all human activity. This is best illustrated by the following example, which posits the divine potential where it might be least expected, in the body. St. Irenaeus of Lyons, who lived in the second century and has come to be appreciated by modern scholars as one of the first great Christian thinkers, insisted that it was precisely our physical shape and form that was patterned according to the image of God. He feared that the over-spiritualizing tendencies of the so-called gnostics (whom we mentioned earlier) would lead to utter denigration of the human body and consequently of human activity, and so he insisted in response to them that the body could be holy and good, and is indisputably capable of salvation.

But how could he insist that the human body is patterned upon a formless God, who has neither shape nor form? St. Irenaeus pointed to Genesis 1:26-27 and contended that we are not the image of God, but made *in* or *according to* the image of God, and that the image of God is none other than Jesus Christ. Even if Christ's body is chronologically posterior to the first human, he is the eternal Son whose incarnation was eternally in the plan of God. St. Irenaeus characterizes us as being only "lately created … having been formed after [Jesus'] likeness, predestinated, according to the pre-science of the Father, that we, who had as yet no exis-tence, might come into being."[9] He suggested that this truth of our formation was taken on faith, so to speak, until Jesus appeared. "For in times long past, it was *said* that man was created after the image of God, but it was not actually *shown* … When, however, the Word of God became flesh, he confirmed [this]."[10] Christ's advent reassured the human race that its creation was indeed very good.

Irenaeus' astonishing declaration concerning the body was intended to proclaim that the *entire* human person, and thus *all* of human activity was modeled on the divine image, and that therefore salvation could not be restricted to a single aspect of human existence as his gnostic opponents contended.

> For by the hands of the Father, that is, by the Son and the Holy Spirit, man, and not merely a part of man, was made in the likeness of God. Now the soul and the spirit are certainly a part of the man, but certainly not the man; for the perfect man consists in the commingling and the union of the soul receiving the spirit of the Father, and the admixture of that fleshly nature which was molded after the image of God.[11]

Irenaeus insisted that fleshly nature or existence is not to be escaped but transfigured by performing spiritual deeds. One does not become spiritual by abandoning hu-man activity, but by transforming it. This is why he says,

> In like manner we do also hear many brethren in the Church, who possess prophetic gifts … whom also the apostle terms "spiritual," they being spiritual because they partake of the Spirit, and not because their flesh has been stripped off and taken away, and because

they have become purely spiritual.[12]

Following Irenaeus, we may conclude that we do not become spiritual by stripping away our professional or social life, but by making both participate in the Spirit. It is the Spirit which allows us to give witness to Christ (Acts 1:8), and we can only give that witness in our activities and daily life, not apart from it.

Christian mystical theology also shows that our imperfection and mutability are neither problems nor cause for chastisement. Imperfection characterizes our condition, for "inasmuch as [we] are not uncreated, for this very reason do [we] come short of the perfect."[13] Mutability allows us to change and pursue the end revealed by Jesus Christ, that is, life in the eternal presence of God. What might appear to be a problem is actually a blessing! So it is with vocation. Searching for our vocation is not a problem that we must confront; it is an opportunity to grow and mature, motivated by the potential revealed to us by Jesus Christ, the New Adam. St. Paul says that "We all reflect as in a mirror the splendor of the Lord; thus we are transfigured into his likeness, from splendor to splendor: such is the influence of the Lord who is Spirit" (2 Cor 3:18). The first Adam suggests possibilities both good and bad, but the last Adam confirms the spiritual splendor of redeemed human nature (cf. 1 Cor 15:45-49). We have the potential to reflect the splendor of the Lord (not of Adam), for it is Jesus of Nazareth who revealed to the world the fulfillment of our potential or the ideal human condition, one that is in perfect communion with God. He reveals this potential because he is the very image of God (Col 1:15), according to which we have been created.

Transformed by Love...

Once we recognize our goal, we can begin the process of transformation. Theophilus spoke of this transformation in an electrifying manner, saying, "If [Adam] were to turn to the life of immortality by keeping the commandment of God, he would win immortality as a reward from him and would become a god."[14] This potential, however, can only be fulfilled if we eagerly embrace it, and so Christian mysticism is also characterized by the concept of a mystical union with God in love. Likewise, the vocational pursuit must be motivated and informed by the individual person's will and desire. What God has made possible for us cannot obscure the centrality of human will, response, and initiative.

At the heart of all Christian theology is the belief that one's approach to God must be free and willing. St. Irenaeus says, "God made man a free agent from the beginning, possessing his own power, even as he does his own soul, to obey the behests of God voluntarily, and not by compulsion of God."[15] If you were to fulfill the behest of God by compulsion, you would be reduced to the level of an automaton. Fulfilling God's commands would be devoid of any personal value or significance if it did not involve any personal commitment to the good. Otherwise, warns St. Irenaeus,

> their being god would be of no consequence, because they were so by nature rather than by will, and are possessors of good spontaneously, not by choice; and for this reason they would not understand that fact, that good is a comely thing, nor would they take pleasure in it.[16]

This good of which Irenaeus speaks we must do voluntarily, lovingly, and with pleasure, for we could not possibly reflect God to others were we to do it grudgingly. God did not call the children of Abraham, Isaac, and Jacob out of Egypt merely to be obedient or submissive. He called them to reestablish his relationship with them and a relationship succeeds only when both parties desire it. This is why he reminded them of his name (Exod 3:14), called them out to the desert to worship him (Exod 5:1), and restored them to a land where they could maintain this relationship (Josh 1:1-9).

We are not predetermined to a specific course or manner of life; rather we have the gift of self-determination and can choose or refuse that which life presents us within parameters far broader than any other creature of this world. One could argue that political, social, and economic obstacles undermine this notion of self-determination and cite as proof the pervasive discrimination against various groups in society. Yet our very awareness of, and concern for, them testifies to the belief that there is potential for change, self-direction, and a rejection of status quo. Why bother documenting injustice if it we indeed lack a free will that could do something about it? This freedom, however, is best conceived in tandem with the process of sanctification of the human body described earlier by St. Irenaeus. Human freedom does not imply abandon, but the ability to make our own ultimate choice, to choose either an animal life confined to this creation, or a truly human life bridging this creation with the Uncreated.

As the human will is sanctified, it learns to function at its optimal capacity by loving the good and acting upon this love. In short, it becomes receptive to the divine. Early Christian theologians often spoke of the fulfillment of our potential in terms of reception, that is, receiving divine life from God and reflecting it to others. The first gift received is often described as that of sonship. St. Paul said that God begins the process of sanctification by making us daughters and sons by adoption, holding us in the same esteem and love as that in which he held Jesus, a Son by nature. The status that he held by nature, we may obtain by adoption; what he was in reality, God chose to make us if we choose to comply and become so by imitation. Many of the theologians from antiquity mentioned in this paper reflected upon this ennobling gift and ebulliently described the blessings derived from it: kinship with God and the dwelling of the Holy Spirit within us! We radiate grace, incorruption, and immortality by acquiring a relationship that nature did not endow and her parameters did not allow. By being adopted, we are given the opportunity to transcend our nature's limitation and a new reality commences.

...into Children of God

This reception of divine life requires human reciprocity. We become God's beloved children from the start because he loved us and justified us through his Son, but we must respond to the Son's work by loving God in return and accepting the Holy Spirit he sends us. But how does one love God? In the same way that God has loved us, by emptying ourselves for his sake. We should love our Heavenly Father as purely as Jesus did, especially when we find ourselves in our own garden of Gethsemane. This is the manner in which we can be glorified as the Son was glorified. St. Cyril of Alexandria, a bishop and theologian of the fifth century, spoke vividly about the Son's glorification.

> Glory is equivalent to the cross. For if at the time of his passion he willingly endured many insults with forbearance, and accepted suffering voluntarily for our sake when it was in his power to avoid it, this acceptance of suffering for the good of others is a sign of extraordinary compassion and the highest glory... When [Jesus] says, 'Glorify thy Son (John 12:27),' he means, 'Allow me to suffer in a voluntary fashion.'[17]

Elsewhere he added that Jesus said "Glorify thy Son," so that "we should pray not to fall into temptation, but if we do fall into it to bear it courageously and not to sidestep it but to pray to God to be saved... For if it is the case that God is glorified through the dangers that threaten us, let all things be considered secondary to that end."[18] Nothing should separate us from our love for Christ (cf. Rom 8:35).

Reflect for a moment upon what this implies for our new, transcendent status. Our glorification and elevation will mimic that of Jesus' glorification and elevation upon the cross; if we are to become like the Son, we too must be willing to love as earnestly as he, even if that means we must give our life for the life of another (Rom 5:7-8). In doing so, we will thus begin to live according to the law of grace, as it was coined by St. Maximus the Confessor, a theologian who lived in the seventh century. Unlike the natural law which you fulfill by doing unto others as you would have them do unto you, or the scriptural law, which you fulfill when you love others as yourself, the law of grace is fulfilled only when you love your neighbor more than yourself and are willing to give your life in exchange, for this is truly like God and an imitation of Jesus of Nazareth.[19] When we love so much that we live and die as Christ would, then we have been truly conformed to Christ (Rom 8:29, 12.2), and we become capable of enjoying our intimate relationship with God in the manner of Jesus. God loves all his children, but those whose hearts are hardened or full of malice derive no pleasure from such knowledge. Yet if we conform ourselves to Jesus, we become like him and call upon God as our own Father. Just as he is the Son by nature, we become daughters and sons by adoption; just as the Son condescended to become human and dwell among us, we are invited to become gods, that is daughters and sons of God standing in his immediate presence (Ps 82:6, Job 1:6, 2 Thess 1:9, Jude 24, Rev 7:15).

Our discussion here revolves around nothing less than everyone's *ultimate* vocation, and it is this ultimate vocation that enriches the present vocational search. Our professional, personal, and social commitments can all be conformed to Christ if we seek ways of glorifying him in even the most mundane task, which can be transformed into an opportunity to manifest God's love to others. One cannot overemphasize the deeply held Christian conviction that *all* our activities should function this way. St. Symeon the New Theologian, a medieval mystic, shocked his audience out of their complacency by speaking of this conformity to Christ in physical imagery that he inherited from his predecessor Irenaeus, but which he developed in a startlingly fresh way. He rapturously exclaimed,

> We become members of Christ – and Christ becomes our members, Christ becomes my hand, Christ, my miserable foot; and I, unhappy one, am Christ's hand, Christ's foot! I move my hand, and my hand is the whole Christ, since do not forget it, God is indivisible in his divinity.[20]

This is not pantheism, a belief that Orthodox theology vigorously rejects. St. Symeon spoke within a larger context of ethical concern and he admonished his audience to a Christian life of faith, commitment, and effort. This is why he immediately added,

> Do not accuse me of blasphemy, but welcome these things and adore Christ who makes you such, since if you so wish you will become a member of Christ and similarly all our members individually and all which is dishonorable in us he will make honorable by adorning it with his divine beauty and his divine glory.[21]

Your eyes, ears, hands, and feet become Christ's, or Christ himself, as Symeon would insist, when your thoughts and deeds are conformed to Christ. Symeon uses all-encompassing imagery to remind each of us that conforming to Christ is a comprehensive transformation.

Truly Brothers and Sisters

If our ultimate vocation is to love as Jesus loved, we cannot be conformed to Christ in isolation from others. One must dispose of the popular image of a mystic as one secluded from society and engaged in a solitary endeavor, and recognize that we must reflect God's glory corporately, too. This is why Jesus prays that his disciples will be found to be one in him, just as he is one with the Father (John 17). St. Paul repeatedly exhorts and admonishes his congregations that they recognize how they now live in Christ with one another and that this reflects the glory of God to others around them (Gal 3:25-29). St. Ignatius of Antioch, whose writings are among the earliest Christian legacy after the

New Testament, also insisted upon this vision for the church. He writes,

> You must join this chorus, every one of you, so that by being harmonious in unanimity and taking your pitch from God you may sing in unison with one voice through Jesus Christ to the Father, in order that he may both hear you and, on the basis of what you do well, acknowledge that you are members of his Son. It is, therefore, advantageous for you to be in perfect unity, in order that you may always have a share in God.[22]

In the church, we realize our union with one another in Christ by living for the other. This completes our adoption by placing us in the same communion with God as that which Christ enjoys, and paves the way for our union with God.

Where others today lose hope for real substantive change or reform in society, we should remind ourselves that we could make a start of it, just as Jesus did with his disciples. The perfect society may only be achieved in the next age, but until then we must accomplish as much as possible to achieve the vision of Jesus, who prayed for the unity of his disciples, that they may be

> bound together tightly with an unbreakable bond of love, that they may advance to such a degree of unity that their freely chosen association might even become an image of the natural unity that is conceived to exist between the Father and Son.[23]

As a body, we are called to form an entity that manifests God's glory to the world, by its unity, harmony, and sacrificial love for the world. Christian faith professes that all of this creation – the world around us, our society, you and I – are capable of manifesting God's glory and goodness. Our innumerable shortcomings repeatedly obstruct the fulfillment of this goal, but there are always imperfect glimpses that manifest themselves and assure us of its possibility in this age and its certainty in the next.

A Summation

Our ultimate vocation is to love the other so that we might reflect God's glory. We must discover and create ways for ourselves to integrate this insight into our own professional lives, so that we might be conformed unto Christ more perfectly. To reject this principle is to abandon the vision of the early Church.

Where others in the ancient world saw a human body that was ever susceptible to harm and illness, a body that was capable of having its life extinguished at any moment, Christians such as Irenaeus saw a body that was "fit for and capable of receiving the power of God, which at the beginning received the skillful touches of God"[24] and which could participate in "the constructive wisdom and power of God."[25] How we participate in that wisdom and power will be determined by each of us in our own life, and our uniqueness demands that the manner chosen will be different from that chosen by everyone else. God's glory is inexhaustible, and so are the possibilities for each of us to be conformed to Christ.

Our vocation is to transform our profession according to the freedom that has been entrusted to us in Christ and the love and compassion we have cultivated for our neighbor (Gal 5:13, 1 Pet 2:16). It is a personal choice, but one of cosmic significance. "For the creation waits with eager longing for the revealing of the sons of God

... because the creation itself will be set free from its bondage to decay and obtain the glorious liberty of the children of God" (Rom 8:19-21).

Notes

1 Two characteristic statements that express this sentiment: Sergei Bulgakov writes "The whole life of Orthodoxy is bound up with visions of the other world. Without that vision Orthodoxy would not exist," in his chapter "Orthodox Mysticism," in *The Orthodox Church* (New York: Morehouse Publishing Co, 1935), 168; see also Kallistos Ware's entry "Eastern Christianity" in Mircea Eliade, ed., *The Encyclopedia of Religion*, vol. 4 (New York: Macmillan Publishing Company, 1987), 570, where he writes, "The bond between theology and prayer is heavily emphasized in Orthodoxy. Theology is seen not merely as an academic or scholarly pursuit, but as preeminently mystical and liturgical."

2 G. Bornkamm, *"mysterion"*, in Gerhard Kittel, ed., *Theological Dictionary of the New Testament*, trans. Geoffrey W. Bromiley (Grand Rapids, MI: Wm. B. Eerdmans, 1967); Louis Dupré and James A. Wiseman, *Light from Light: An Anthology of Christian Mysticism* (New York: Paulist Press, 1988), 3-26.

3 Dupré and Wiseman, *Light from Light*, 9-12; see also Andrew Louth, *The Origins of the Christian Mystical Tradition* (Oxford: Clarendon Press, 1981).

4 The theology of the image has been dismissed as a patristic construct and not genuinely scriptural theology, because the references to it in Scripture are few and they remained undeveloped until the introduction of Greek language and philosophy (particularly Stoic and Platonic) in the Hellenistic and Late Roman periods. Orthodox scholars in the past and present have rebutted that the theology of the image is characteristically scriptural, and not Greek. See Vladimir Lossky, "The Theology of the Image" in idem, *In the Image and Likeness of God* (Crestwood, NY: St. Vladimir's Seminary Press, 1985) 125-137. Lossky argues that God is totally other, yet he chose to enter into personal relationships with us and call us by name, a notion that was folly to the Greek mind, which would never have granted any attributes to the truly transcendent. He

also argues that the theology of the image could never have been developed apart from the complete revelation of Jesus as the image of the Father, a revelation that introduced the distinction between nature and person, and taught us that human beings are not simply an individuated nature, but persons related to God singly and uniquely, each one enjoying a unique relationship with him. See also Eugen J. Pentiuc, *Jesus the Messiah in the Hebrew Bible* (Paulist Press, 2005), which reasserts the significance of the image of God within its original setting, by offering a penetrating interpretation derived from a rhetorical and linguistic analysis of the Hebrew text.

5 Theophilus of Antioch *Ad Autolycum* 2.24, trans. Robert McQueen Grant, *Ad Autolycum* (Oxford: Clarendon Press, 1970). All subsequent citations are from this translation.

6 Theophilus of Antioch *Ad Autolycum* 2.24.

7 Christoph Markschies, *Gnosis: An Introduction* (London: T&T Clark, 2003); Hans Jonas, *The Gnostic Religion: The Message of the Alien God and the Beginnings of Christianity* (Boston: Beacon Press, 2001); Giovanni Filoramo, *A History of Gnosticism*, trans. Anthony Alcock (Malden, MA: Blackwell Publishers, 1990).

8 See the final hymn of the aposticha (plagal fourth tone), an English translation of which is available in *The Lenten Triodion*, trans. Mother Mary and Archimandrite Kallistos Ware (London: Faber and Faber, 1978), 516.

9 Irenaeus *Against Heresies* 5.1.1, in *Ante-Nicene Fathers*, vol. 1, ed. Alexander Roberts, James Donaldson, and A. Cleveland Coxe, (New York: Christian Literature Company, 1890; reprint, Grand Rapids, MI: W.B. Eerdmans, 1965). All subsequent citations are from this translation.

10 Irenaeus *Against Heresies* 5.16.2.

11 Irenaeus *Against Heresies* 5.6.1.

12 Irenaeus *Against Heresies* 5.6.1.

13 Irenaeus *Against Heresies* 4.38.1.

14 Theophilus of Antioch *Ad Autolycum* 2.27.

15 Irenaeus *Against Heresies* 4.37.1.

16 Irenaeus *Against Heresies* 4.37.6.

17 Cyril of Alexandria *Commentary on John* 8, trans. Norman Russell, *Cyril of Alexandria* (London: Routledge, 2000), 121.

18 Ibid.

19 Maximus the Confessor *Ad Thalassium* 64; an English translation is available in *On the Cosmic Mystery of Jesus Christ: Selected Writings from St. Maximus the Confessor*, trans. Paul M. Blowers and Robert Louis Wilken (Crestwood, NY: St. Vladimir's Seminary Press, 2003), 145-171.

20 Symeon the New Theologian *Hymn 15*, trans. George A. Maloney, *Hymns of Divine Love* (Denville, NJ: Dimension Books, 1976), 51-57.

21 Ibid.

22 Ignatius *Letter to Ephesians* 4.2, trans. Robert M. Grant, *The Apostolic Fathers: A New Translation and Commentary* (New York: T. Nelson, 1968).

23 Cyril of Alexandria *Commentary on John* 11.9, in Russell, *Cyril of Alexandria*, 128.

24 Irenaeus *Against Heresies* 5.2.2.

25 Irenaeus *Against Heresies* 5.3.2.

The Call of the Virgin Mary

Deborah Malacky Belonick

Introduction

Meditating upon the life of the Virgin Mary, I want to reflect upon eight specific points of hearing God's call. I use her as an example for all human beings, because what happened in her life certainly will find its counterpart in every Christian born of the Spirit of God.[1] Though not called to be the mother of God, we are called to a life that is lived in relation to God, a life that is hidden with Christ in God (Col 3:3). Many gospel passages involving Mary reveal invaluable lessons about this consecrated life, about vocation within the body of Christ as distinguished from natural abilities that lead to a particular profession or occupation.

God calls single-minded persons of integrity.

> Now in the sixth month the angel Gabriel was sent by God to a town in Galilee called Nazareth, to a **virgin** engaged to a man whose name was Joseph, of the house of David. (Luke 1:26–27)

Mary was "a virgin." Her virginity implied more than the absence of sexual experience – often errantly viewed as a "deficiency" in our contemporary culture. Rather, her bodily integrity signified her internal purity, her "undisturbed orientation of the whole personal life towards God, in complete self-dedication."[2]

Twentieth-century theologian Georges Florovsky explained this venerable connotation:

> Now virginity is not simply a bodily status or a physical feature as such. Above all it is a spiritual and inner attitude, and apart from that, a bodily status would be altogether meaningless...[3]

Integrity, wholeness, and purposeful dedication: these mark the characteristics of the virginity of the Theotokos,[4] who offered her entire being to God to fulfill her vocation. Like her, we must at least *discover* our entire being and then offer it as a sacrifice to God, to let him do his work in us.

In our highly sexualized culture, we may offer part of our bodies and part of our hearts to many people – and we may subsequently feel disintegration, even boredom or callousness, from these casual encounters. Operating in a piecemeal manner, not just sexually but also relationally, both to other people and to our work, sets us adrift, tethered to earth *and* sky by very thin threads. Such shallow relationships with others and with God result in an impoverished emotional life: neither deep love nor deep hate wells up in the chest. As passionate beings, we scatter our energies among many projects, all of which feel equally meaningless: an air of depression, a sense of loss, and a constant hunger pervades.

I have been there. I remember going to the confessional in my youth and admitting with extreme sadness, "Father, I just don't know where I belong, or why

I am here."

The remedy for this sense of alienation, this sense of "not belonging," begins, oddly enough, with an internal realignment – an initial, gentle acceptance of the "good, bad, and ugly" within one's own center. It begins with the loving and courageous exploration of the heart.

St. Makarios, a fourth-century ascetic of the Egyptian desert, noted,

> ...Within the heart are unfathomable depths. There are reception rooms and bedchambers in it, doors and porches, and many offices and passages...The heart is a small vessel: and yet dragons and lions are there, and there poisonous creatures and all the treasures of wickedness; rough, uneven paths are there, and gaping chasms. There likewise is God, there are the angels, there life and the Kingdom, there light and the apostles, the heavenly cities and the treasures of grace: all things are there.[5]

Willingness to engage our own emotions within the chambers of our heart is the first step to becoming integral, virginal. This process involves not repression – a dangerous spiritual mistake[6] – but honest acknowledgement and struggle.

When characters in the Gospels met Jesus Christ, they simultaneously came face-to-face with themselves. The rich, young ruler found he had a stronger attachment to money than to God (Luke 18:18–30). The woman at Jacob's Well found she was more attached to men than to God (John 4:1–42). The Apostle Peter found he was more attached to security and fame than to God (Mark 8:31–38). All of these wanted a religious answer or a theological formula to solve their problems. They all very much wanted to fit into a religious system. But

Christ's probing admonitions instead forced them to face and deal with the dragons lurking in their hearts.

Finding one's vocation is not an analytical exercise, but rather a face-to-face encounter with the living God. The deadly serious business of piercing the heart involves letting Jesus Christ walk through every chamber, every passage, every room, until he transforms them all and a true "cleansing of the Temple" of our body and soul takes place (Mark 11:15–18; 1 Cor 3:16). Let us not mistake how this is done: the work of cleansing the temple is his; the work of opening the door to that temple is ours (Rev 3:20).

Vocation is more about being than doing.

The virgin's **name** was **Mary**. (Luke 1:27)

It is a truism that our vocation will depend on our character, our reputation not only among our fellow human beings but also our reputation according to God's all-seeing eye. Scripture tells us that we all have an identity before God that mirrors our life in Christ Jesus. The names of people in Scripture often reveal their character: "Abraham" literally means "father of a great multitude"; "David" means "well-beloved, dear"; "Esther" means "secret, hidden." The names of all of these biblical figures reveal their moral fiber, which essentially was tied to their vocation. The name "Mary," in Hebrew *Miriam*, means "sea of bitterness," and the Virgin's name describes her trials as she fulfilled her vocation as the mother of God.

I once had a professor of dogmatic theology[7] who taught me a great lesson about vocation. When speaking to our class about ordination to the priesthood, he observed (in his charming Russian accent): "I am a lay-person, and I always will be a layperson. It does not matter how many times some bishop would place his hands on my head to say the prayer of ordination – I still would remain a layperson!"

Sacraments are not magic: they are the gifts that transform – or rather, transport – natural life to life as it exists in God's kingdom, life within his mind's eye and purpose. We can strive for any vocation, but if our personality and character do not fulfill that calling – if we are not suited to the mystery – our discontent becomes a thorn to those around us.

God rarely will tell us explicitly what to do. Rather, he will reveal to us who he is. Likewise, our vocation has more to do with our being than our doing. The condition of our character and our relationship to God will determine our vocation – neither our natural abilities nor our preferences are factors. These may be determinative for our professions, but not for our vocations, which are determined by the degree in which we dwell in Christ and by the degree in which his nature indwells us. "The most important aspect of Christianity is not the work we do, but the relationship we maintain [with Jesus Christ] and the surrounding influence and qualities produced by that relationship. That is all God wants us to give our attention to, and it is the one thing that is continually under attack."[8]

What God demands initially and foremost is our very selves, not our time or talents. He demands a surrender of our human will, so that the divine nature that dwelt in his Son would dwell in us. It is by developing a family resemblance to Jesus that we find our vocation. The Book of Revelation says that in the kingdom true believers will share the secret name of Jesus Christ, which no one can learn without sharing in his suffering and divine life (Rev 2:17; 3:12; 14:3). In this world, believers bearing Christ will automatically, without conscious reflection – in relationships and in their daily tasks – bear the divine family name and do the work of the Father in heaven (John 10:37–38; 14:12).

God prepares a person for a vocation.

And he came to her and said, "Greetings **favored one**! The Lord is with you." But she was much perplexed by his words, and pondered what sort of greeting this might be. (Luke 1:28–29)

The angel Gabriel came to the Virgin Mary to tell her that she had been chosen for a particular vocation. The Greek phrase "full of grace," or "favored one" (*kecharitōmenē*), places the emphasis not on Mary, but on God: she is the object of God's grace and favor. In fact, the participial form indicates that Mary has been chosen for a long time past; God's full flow of favor has been concentrated on her.[9] This was God's plan, not Mary's plan, and he had prepared her for it.

St. John of Damascus, who collated and epitomized the opinions of the great ecclesiastical writers who had gone before him, describes Mary's preparatory years:

She was predestined in the eternal foreknowing counsel of God and she was prefigured by various figures and foretold by the Holy Ghost through the words of the prophets…And she was born in the house of Joachim at the Probatica and was brought to the Temple. From then on she grew up in the house of God, nourished by the Spirit, and like a fruitful olive tree (Ps 51:10) became an abode of every virtue with her mind removed from every worldly and carnal desire.[10]

God had prepared Mary through the generations preceding her. But in her genealogy – recorded in Matthew and Luke through the line of her betrothed, Joseph, to whose ancestry she also belonged[11] – one does not find particularly illustrious people: there are wicked kings, murderers, adulterers, prostitutes, and apostates. Yet, throughout the successive generations, God was smoothing off these rough-hewn humans, teaching and disciplining these people, until Mary "full of grace" was born.

The Orthodox tradition bears witness to the notion that Mary had an idyllic upbringing, one that would prepare her to become the Lord's mother. However, less than idyllic childhoods, less than idyllic lives, still can lead to wonderful vocations.

Elizaveta Pilenko, today canonized as Mother Maria Skobtsova, was born in 1891 into an aristocratic family in Riga, Latvia. Her eclectic lifestyle included her among the literary intelligentsia and the Socialist Revolutionary Party. She married at a young age within this social circle and bore a daughter, but her marriage collapsed within three years. When the Bolsheviks overthrew the government in October 1917, she left for Anapa on the Black Sea coast and there served as mayor. There, this divorced, passionate young woman married again, this time to an anti-Bolshevik officer. In 1923, threatened with assassination, she joined the throng of refugees uprooted by revolution and civil war and made her way to France. By then, she was pregnant with a third child.

She lost a daughter to meningitis, a tragedy that initiated a profound experience of repentance. She and her second husband, who had met and impetuously married in the abnormal setting of the Russian civil war, parted and divorced on amiable terms. This second failed marriage providentially opened the way for her to become a professed nun in 1932. At this point, her monastic profession took on a unique dimension. Immersing herself in efforts to assist destitute Russian refugees, she sought them out in prisons, hospitals, mental asylums, and in the slums. Increasingly, she emphasized the religious dimension of this work, the insight that "each person is the very icon of God incarnate in the world."[12] She became a maternal figure, "Mother Maria," to all who needed care, and during the Nazi occupation of France, she assisted and rescued Jews.

Eventually, because of her resistance activities, she was sent to the notorious Ravensbrück women's concentration camp north of Berlin. Mother Maria managed to survive almost to the war's end, all the while caring for the bodies and souls of her fellow prisoners. In captivity, she occasionally traded bread for needle and thread in order to embroider religious images that gave her strength. Her last work of art was an embroidered icon of Mary the Mother of God holding the child Jesus, his hands and feet already bearing the wounds of the Cross.

On Good Friday, March 31, 1945, with the gunfire of approaching Russian troops audible in the distance, Mother Maria took the place of a Jewish prisoner who was to be sent to the gas chamber and died in her place.[13]

God prepares people, even through adversity. Mother Maria's life took twists and turns, many of which were fraught with suffering – but the suffering honed her character and shaped her vocation.

Thus, through joyous and tragic experiences, God

shapes our vocations. A poem by Grant Colfax Tuller expresses this beautifully:

> My life is but a weaving betwixt my God and me;
> I do not choose the colors He worketh steadily.
> Oft times He weaveth sorrow, and I in foolish pride
> Forget He sees the upper, and I the underside.
> Not till the loom is silent and the shuttles cease to fly
> Will God unfold the pattern and explain the reason why.
> For the dark threads are as needful in the Weaver's skillful hand
> As the threads of gold and silver in the pattern He has planned.[14]

Mother Gavrilia, an Orthodox nun, presents a reflection that bears striking resemblance to this poem in her biography, *Ascetic of Love*: "Someone was complaining of being unfairly treated…Then one day he had a vision: He saw God, up in Heaven, with an embroidery-frame, on which He was embroidering the lives of all of us. He also saw us humans, down on Earth, looking only at the loose threads hanging from the reverse of the Embroidery, unable to discern or understand God's wonderful Needlework…"[15]

A low point in life does not signal God's abandonment. Proverbs 16:9 states, "A man's heart plans his way, but the Lord directs his steps." Plan we may, but we must be open to the twists and turns that God places in our paths: they are placed there as preparation for our vocation, and for Christ-realization rather than self-realization.

God may or may not explain the purpose of his call.

Then the angel said to her, "Do not be afraid, Mary,

for you have found favor with God. And now, you will conceive in your womb and bear a son, and you will name him Jesus. He will be great, and will be called the Son of the Most High; and the Lord God will give to him the throne of his ancestor David. He will reign over the house of Jacob forever, and of his kingdom there will be no end. Mary said to the angel, **"How can this be, since I am a virgin?"** The angel said to her, **"The Holy Spirit will come upon you, and the power of the Most High will overshadow you; therefore the child to be born will be holy; he will be called the Son of God...for with God, nothing will be impossible."** (Luke 1:30–37)

At the Annunciation, the angel explained God's action and purpose to the Virgin Mary. However, at other times in the Gospels, no immediate explanation is given.

When the young boy Jesus left the company of his extended family during a pilgrimage to Jerusalem, he caused his parents extreme anxiety when they discovered him missing from among their friends and relatives. They found him teaching in the Temple among the elders, and his mother questioned him: "Son, why have you done this to us? Look, your father and I have sought you anxiously" (Luke 2:48).

Jesus replied, "Why did you seek me? Did you not know that I must be about my Father's business?" But the Gospel says that his parents "...did not understand the statement which he spoke to them. Then he went down with them and came to Nazareth, and was subject to them, but his mother kept all these things in her heart" (Luke 2:49–50).

The Virgin Mary often pondered the mystery of her Son and the words uttered by the angel and by her child and the prophecies surrounding him (Luke 2:19,

51). The Greek verb for "kept pondering" (*dielogizeto*) implies intense, prolonged reflection, which activates a strong spirit of faith.[16] Although Mary did not understand all the events surrounding the life of her Son, she meditated on the circumstances and developed an abiding trust in God's purpose.

A person cannot develop faith or trust if given constant clarification. When parents send a freshman off to college, they do not often hear a detailed explanation of what is happening in the dormitory or classroom. E-mails may pass back and forth quite regularly the first few days, but as the freshman becomes more engrossed in college life, the parent begins to experience a drought of information. In the face of this dearth of communication, the parent has to begin to trust that the freshman is alive and flourishing in the new environment. So it is in relation to God. Even though he is not sending us clear messages daily as to his activities and plans, we come to trust that he knows what he is doing and that he has our world under control.

There is a wonderful story of St. Anthony the Great, a fourth-century monk of the Egyptian desert. Legend has it that demons in the guise of wild beasts would appear in Anthony's cell and attack him: "...forms of lions, bears, leopards, bulls, serpents, asps, scorpions, and wolves, and each of them was moving according to his nature."[17] These apparitions brutally tormented Anthony as he prayed through Scripture verses to comfort himself.

After much suffering, Anthony looked up and saw the roof open, and a ray of light descending to him. The demons suddenly vanished, the pain of his body ceased, and the building came back together. Anthony, sensing the presence of Christ and regaining his breath asked, "Where were you, Lord? Why did you not appear at the beginning to make my pains to cease?" And a voice came to him, "Anthony, I was here, but I waited to see how you would fight; wherefore since you have endured, and have not been overcome, I will ever be a helper to you, and will make your name known everywhere."[18]

It is difficult to trust in the character of God during times of distress, perhaps more difficult than enduring the trial at hand. But the Virgin Mary and the saints teach us to cling to the knowledge that God is good and that he is teaching us, even when he is utterly silent.

A call from God, if answered, will bear fruit.

> "Here am I, the servant of the Lord; **let it be** to me according to your word." (Luke 1:38)

Cooperation with a call from God produces fruit. The acceptance of the Virgin Mary of her vocation caused salvation himself to enter the world. Poignant are the words of Metropolitan Philaret of Moscow (1782–1867), who expressed this idea beautifully in a sermon that he gave in honor of the Annunciation:

> During the days of the creation of the world, when God uttered his living and mighty words: *Let there be…* the Creator's words brought creatures into existence. But on the day, unique in the existence of the world, when Holy Mary uttered her humble and obedient *Let it be*, I would hardly dare to express what took place then – the word of the creature caused the Creator to descend into the world…"[19]

Even after the death of the person called, a harvest

from his or her obedience will appear like wheat that springs from a seed buried in the ground.

A person cannot rush God's call.

The story of Jesus and his mother at the wedding in Cana of Galilee illustrates a time when Mary tried to rush God's purpose (John 2:1–12). It seems a simple scene, but there are double meanings throughout the Greek text that indicate Mary is being overbearing and asking for special privileges as Jesus' mother.[20]

Mary, concerned with hospitality, points out to Jesus that the wine is gone. She is noting not only the absence of physical wine, but also an absence of "spiritual wine." In the Bible, wine is a symbol of joy – not joy in drink, which leads to drunkenness, but the joy of being in God's presence. Wine also is often a symbol of God's heavenly banquet, the marriage feast of the kingdom to come (Rev 19:7–9; cf. Mat 22:2–14; Luke 12:36–37).[21] When Mary says, "**They have no wine**" (John 2:3), she could be intimating, "They have no joy *in their spirits*, no joy *of the Spirit*. Their souls are dry." She looks around at the drunken crowd (for the wine is gone!) and notices their spiritual desolation.[22] Then, she looks to her son for help.

Jesus replies to her, "O, woman what is that to you and me? My hour has not yet come"(John 2:4).[23] Jesus had come to write the law of God on the tablet of the heart, and Mary was the first human being to comprehend and accept this, but she could not rush God and his purpose. At the wedding of Cana, she had to accept what her Son could offer at that moment.[24]

In effect, Jesus curbs Mary's enthusiasm and intention. Some commentators state that in this passage she represents the believing church that awaits the out-pouring of the works of Jesus. She was anticipating the Messianic Age in which, as the prophet Joel foretold, "the mountains shall drip with sweet wine" or "the mountains will run with new wine" (Joel 3:18).

But Jesus cannot bring this to full completion until he has accomplished his mission and returned to his Father (cf. John 14:12–13).[25] He cannot send the Holy Spirit or give the new wine of the kingdom, because he has not yet been crucified and glorified. On Pentecost, *all* the words of Joel will be fulfilled: "… in the last days…I will pour out my Spirit upon all flesh, and your sons and your daughters shall prophesy, and your young men shall see visions, and your old men shall dream dreams" (Joel 3.28). But, for now, he only can give them a foretaste of this joy – sweet wine, ful-filling in part the prophecy.

Zealous Christians often manufacture circumstances to produce a calling, or else they rush God's calling. It is a frequent mistake. Starry-eyed Joseph, motivated by his multicolored coat and dreaming of subservient sheaves of wheat, most likely never imagined an exile and an imprisonment would be required before that vision ma-terialized (Gen 44:26). Sarah made the same error when she got discouraged waiting for a son from her own womb and asked her husband Abraham to impregnate Hagar, her handmaiden (Gen 16:3–4). Peter, just after confessing that Jesus was the Christ, the Son of the liv-ing God, tried to dissuade his Master from going to his death (Mat 16:23). If these chosen people erred in this way, why would we think ourselves exempt from this temptation? Instead of waiting for God's ripe moment, we intrude as little providences and divert God's pur-pose. Discerning a vocation requires utmost patience.

A vocation has a communal impact.

By a reverberating "Yes" to God's invitation at the Annunciation, the Virgin Mary reversed the curse of death and opened a path for Eternal Life to enter the world. At the cross of Jesus, Mary continued her saving role by sharing her motherly relationship to her Son with us.

At the crucifixion, the Virgin Mary and the beloved disciple John stand and mourn Jesus' death on Golgotha. Jesus says to Mary, "Woman, behold your son!" To John he says, **"Behold, your mother!"** (John 19:26–27).

It seems in this scene that Jesus is providing for the care and protection of his mother. However, the sentence structure John uses in this particular passage indicates that Mary is also being given to the community of believers. John 19:27 states: "And from that hour the disciple took her to his own home." In Greek, the phrase "to his own home" is *eis ta ithia,* the same phrase used in John 1:11, "The true light that enlightens every man was coming into the world. He came *to his own* and his own received him not" [emphasis mine].

This parallel hardly can be accidental.[26] The beloved John did not take Mary into just his own home, but to *his own,* meaning the community of the new covenant. She was to be their mother as well as his. When Jesus gave up his spirit, his pierced side spilled forth blood and water. These were the signs of the new covenant, baptism and the Eucharist, sacraments that would nourish the infant church. However, before his death, Jesus also gave the church a mother, his own mother, to protect and succor it.

According to Christian legend, after the resurrection

and ascension of Christ, the Virgin Mary remained on earth for at least a decade, teaching about the new faith, encouraging the believers, and interceding for the foundling church.[27] In heaven, she intercedes with audacity and love for us before her son Jesus Christ.[28]

Christianity is a communal religion. There is a Russian adage: "We are saved together, we perish alone." Jesus said, "Love one another, as I have loved you" (Jn 13:34). St. Paul said, "I have become all things to all men in order that by all means I might save some" (1 Cor 9:22). Orthodox Christians plead, "Most Holy Theotokos, save us," in the Divine Liturgy, since we are involved in "saving" each other (1 Cor 7:16). Salvation is a corporate enterprise; working out salvation in Christ Jesus demands community.

And, so it has been from the beginning. In the Book of Genesis, the story of creation, the woman is described as a "helper fit" (in Hebrew, *ezer ke neg do*), for the man whom God had formed (Gen 2:20–23). Often this female "helper" is imagined as retainer, an employee, domestic help, or as a mother's or teacher's helper. On the contrary, the Hebrew verb *'azar*, from which the noun *'ezer* derives, means 'to succor' (at the existential level of being), to 'save from extremity,' 'to deliver from death.' In other Semitic languages, it describes the action of someone who gives water to a person dying of thirst or who places a tourniquet on the arm of a bleeding man, thereby saving his life. Thus, far from being a subordinate or menial servant, woman is the savior of man."[29] In the Garden of Eden, Eve was created to save Adam from isolation, alienation, and egoism, and to create human community.

Vocation involves relationships: being father, mother, wife, husband, sister, and brother, not only to our blood relatives, but also to our family members in Christ Jesus. Community shapes vocations, and development of vocations requires community.

As the magnitude of the vocation increases, so does the preparation.

"The sword" referred to in the Gospel of Luke, in the scene in which Mary presents her eight-day-old son to God in the Temple, offers another powerful lesson about vocation.

> Then Simeon blessed them, and said to Mary his mother, "Behold, this Child is destined for the fall and rising of many in Israel, and for a sign which will be spoken against (yes, a **sword** will pierce through your own soul also)...." (Luke 2:34–35)

What is this sword? Fourth-century bishop St. Basil the Great (c. 330–379) says it is the "word that tries and judges our thoughts, which pierces even to the dividing asunder of soul and spirit and of the joints and marrow, and is a discerner of our thoughts."[30]

St. Basil maintained that at the cross, at the hour of Jesus' passion, every soul was subjected to a kind of searching. Mary herself, standing by the cross – even though she had long ago heard the voice of Gabriel and been privy to the secret mystery of the divine conception – felt in her soul "a mighty tempest."[31] Mary herself, beholding what was being done to her son and hearing the chorus of mocking voices around her, reached a moment of doubt. The "sword" of which Simeon spoke so many years before had opened her heart, and there lay a vestige of the "old Eve" – "some doubt," says St. Basil. Despite the fact that "a certain swift healing" came from the Lord to Mary following the resurrection, which confirmed her faith in him, there was a dark moment, a time of terror, when her heart contained what all human nature contains: doubt, and the struggle between the old nature and the new nature in Christ Jesus.[32]

Finding one's vocation is a process dependent on growth in the life of Christ. God is a loving but demanding Father, and he will afford opportunities for us to replace our old human nature with the nature that lives in his Son. These opportunities, in many cases, will require that we enter the humiliation and suffering of our Lord Jesus Christ. Mary herself had to bear the humiliation and anguish of seeing her son die on the cross, a necessary step in her communion with him.

Falsely assuming that suffering cannot come from the hand of God, we try to avoid or wriggle out of difficult circumstances with difficult people. We begin to question lofty Gospel passages – "Love your enemies, do good to those who hate you, bless those who curse you, pray for those who mistreat you" (Luke 6:27–28). We begin to reason: "Surely the Lord could not have meant that! I've been unjustly treated and all the people around me are dysfunctional; surely he meant that I should correct them and demand my rights."[33] Little by little, we erode the Gospel message, and little by little, God's call becomes fainter.

The Virgin Mary, struggling to the end with her vocation, overcame all personal temptation. So admirable was her victory that the Eastern Church proclaims her to be "more honorable than the cherubim and more glorious beyond compare than the seraphim."[34]

Concluding remarks

Christian vocation, unlike a profession or job, requires a relationship to Jesus Christ and an infilling of his Spirit. It is tied to personal character; more specifically it is tied to having the character of Jesus Christ himself abiding within. Paradoxically, the stronger his divine nature within us, the more we become ourselves (Luke 9:24). The more we submit our own will to God's will, the more authentic we become; our facade drops and our unique personhood blossoms.

Throughout her life, beginning with her first response to the angel, "Here am I, the servant of the Lord; let it be to me according to your word" (Luke 1:38), the Virgin Mary developed in her vocation. In this development, there were instances when "swords" pierced her soul, culminating in the death of her son at the cross.

By her assent to God's call and her continual obedience to his will, the Virgin Mary reversed the downward spiral of humanity toward darkness and death, and she fulfilled her unique vocation. Through our own assent to God's call and obedience to him, we also enter into a new life in Christ, and we discover our vocation within his body.[35]

It is a great honor to be called by God for a purpose, a mercy beyond measure, but this call also entails discernment and extreme humility. What does God demand of us? Our very selves, remade in accordance with his will and nature. What does God give back to us? A life that shouts, "My spirit rejoices in God my Savior" (Luke 1:47).

Notes

1 "Throughout most of the history of Christian education, at least until the Reformation, the lives of the saints served as patterns of character, and among these the life of Mary occupied a unique position, corresponding to the unique position she had occupied in the plan of God ... [Her virtues] were there not only to be admired and cherished but *to be imitated.*" [emphasis added] Jaroslav Jan Pelikan, *Mary through the Centuries: Her Place in the History of Culture* (New Haven, CT: Yale University Press, 1996), 220–221. Cf. Oswald Chambers, who expresses well the notion that the way of salvation open to Mary and the process of working out salvation is open also to us. *Daily Thoughts for Disciples* (Grand Rapids, MI: Discovery House Publishers, 1976, 1994), December 28; cf. *God's Workmanship*, 63.

2 Georges Florovsky, *Creation and Redemption: Volume III in the Collected Works* (Belmont, MA: Nordland Publishing Company, 1976), "The Ever-Virgin Mother of God," 184. Cf. 1 Cor 7:34: "...the virgin thinks about the things of the Lord, that she may be holy in body and spirit."

3 *Creation and Redemption*, "The Ever-Virgin Mother of God," 184.

4 Note: The traditional title for the Virgin Mary in the Orthodox Church is *Theotokos*, literally "God bearer," a term that arose during the fifth-century conflict between Nestorius and Cyril of Alexandria and was adopted by the Third Ecumenical Council (Ephesus, 431). Although the Theotokos literally bore God, all believers in fact bear his life, his divine nature, within themselves.

5 Igumen Chariton of Valamo, *The Art of Prayer: An Orthodox Anthology*, E. Kadloubovsky and E. M. Palmer, trans. and Timothy Ware, ed. (London: Faber and Faber Ltd, 1966), 18–19.

6 Conrad W. Baars, *Feeling and Healing Your Emotions* (Gainesville, FL: Bridge-Logos Publishers, 1997). Dr. Baars, a Roman Catholic psychiatrist, writes on "affirmation therapy" and the healing of the whole person – body, mind, and spirit.

7 Sergius S. Verhovskoy was professor of Dogmatic, Moral, and Comparative Theology at St. Vladimir's Orthodox Theological Seminary, Crestwood, NY from 1952 to 1981.

8 Oswald Chambers, *My Utmost for His Highest*, James Reimann, ed. (Grand Rapids, MI: Discovery House Publishers, 1992), August 4.

9 *The Jerome Biblical Commentary*, Raymond E. Brown, ed. (Englewood Cliffs, NJ: Prentice Hall, Inc., 1968), 122. Brown notes: "P. Joüon translated the passage: 'I salute you, object of [divine] favor.' (*NRT* 66 [1939] 797)."

10 *The Fathers of the Church: Saint John of Damascus Writings*, Frederic H. Chase, Jr., trans. (Washington D.C.: The Catholic University of America Press, Inc., 1958, 1970), 362–363.

11 Ibid., 362: "…it was not customary for the Hebrews, nor for sacred Scripture either, to give the pedigrees of women. But there was a law that one tribe should not marry into another. And Joseph, who was descended from the tribe of David and was a just man, for the holy Gospel testifies to this in his regard, would not have espoused the blessed Virgin illegally, but only if she were descended from the same tribe. Consequently it was sufficient to show the descent of Joseph."

12 Jim Forest, "Mother Maria Skobtsova: Nun and Martyr." September 9, 1998 <http://ourworld.compuserve.com/homepages/jim_forest/mmaria.htm>. The text about Mother Maria is taken from *The Ladder of the Beatitudes* (Orbis Books, 1988).

13 Ibid., Cf. Sergei Hackel, *Pearl of Great Price: The Life of Mother Maria Skobtsova 1891–1945* (Crestwood, NY: St. Vladimir's Seminary Press, 1981).

14 Tuller was a twentieth-century Protestant composer of gospel hymns, and although this poem appears on the web site: <http://www.backtothebible.org/gateway/today.htm/20097>, I have not been able to find the original publisher.

15 *The Ascetic of Love: Mother Gavrilia (1897–1992)*, Helen Anthony, trans. (Athens: Eptalofos Sa, 1999, 2000), 309.

16 *Jerome Biblical Commentary*, 122.

17 *Early Church Fathers* (*Nicene and Post-Nicene Fathers* [NPNF] Series II, vol. IV) http://www.ccel.org/fathers2/NPNF2-04/Npnf2-04-38.htm.

18 Ibid.

19 Georges Florovsky, *Creation and Redemption*, "The Ever-Virgin Mother of God," 181.

20 St. John Chrysostom points out several places in the Gospels where the Mother of God claims a maternal privilege and is corrected by her son Jesus. Cf. St. John Chrysostom, *Homily XXII* on the Gospel of John 2:4, in *Nicene and Post-Nicene Fathers: A Select*

Library of the Christian Church (NPNF), Philip Schaff, ed., vol. XIV (Peabody, MA: Hendrickson Publishers, Inc., 1995), 74: "And therefore he answered thus in this place, and again elsewhere, 'Who is my mother, and who are my brethren?' (Matt 12:48), because she, because she had borne him, claimed, according to the custom of other mothers, to direct him in all things, when she ought to have reverenced and worshiped him...otherwise he could not have led up her thoughts from his present lowliness to his future exaltation, and she expected that she should always be honored by him as by a son, and not that he should come as her Master."

21 *The Interpreter's One-Volume Commentary on the Bible*, Charles M. Laymon, ed. (Nashville, TN: Abingdon Press, 1971), 712.

22 "Mary: Model of the Charismatic as Seen in Acts 1–2, Luke 1–2, and John," by René Laurentin in *Mary, the Spirit and the Church*, Vincent P. Branick, S.M., ed. (Ramsey, NJ: Paulist Press, 1980), 40.

23 *The Jerusalem Bible* (Garden City, NY: Doubleday & Co., 1966): "Lit. 'What to me and to thee,' a Semitic formula not infrequent in the OT, Judg 11:12; 2 Sam 16:10, 19:23; 1 Kgs 17:18 and in the NT, Mark 1:24, 5:7; Luke 4:34, 8:28. It is used to deprecate interference, or more strongly, to reject overtures of any kind. The shade of meaning can be deduced only from the context. Here, Jesus objects that his hour has not yet come."

24 Laurentin, "Mary: Model of the Charismatic as Seen in Acts 1–2, Luke 1–2, and John," 39–41.

25 *The Interpreter's One-Volume Commentary on the Bible*, Charles M. Laymon, ed. (Nashville, TN: Abingdon Press, 1971), 712.

26 Andre Feuillet, *Jesus and His Mother* (Still River, MA: St. Bede's Publications, 1974), 209.

27 *The Assumption of our Most Holy Lady, the Mother of God and Ever-Virgin Mary*, trans. from the *Menology of St. Dimitri of Rostov* (Jordanville, NY: St. Job of Pochaev, 1990), 3: "Her age at death was between 57 and 72 years; anywhere from 10 to 19 years after the Ascension of Christ, whom she bore at age 14. Hippolytus claims she died at age 43; Euodus, age 44; Eusebius, 48; and St. Dionysius, who converted in the year A.D. 52, claims to have been at her death. St. Dimitri says the diversity is accounted for by the persecutions of the early Church and consequent difficulties in writing and preserving records."

28 Matthew the Poor, *The Communion of Love* (Crestwood, NY: St.

Vladimir's Seminary Press, 1984), 212–213.

29 Nancy Holloway, *Woman as God-bearer: Maternity and the Mother of God.* Unpublished Doctorate of Ministry thesis, St. Vladimir's Orthodox Theological Seminary, May 1991.

30 *Nicene and Post-Nicene Fathers: A Select Library of the Christian Church* (NPNF), Philip Schaff and Henry Wace, eds., vol. VIII (Peabody, MA: Hendrickson Publishers, Inc., 1995), 298–299; cf. Heb 4:12.

31 Ibid., 299.

32 Ibid., 299. Cf. *Jerome Biblical Commentary*, 125, which notes: "Some of the Church Fathers interpreted the sword as one of doubt or hesitation in faith (so Origen, Chrysostom, Basil, Cyril of Alexandria)…"

33 Cf. Dietrich Bonhoeffer, *The Cost of Discipleship* (New York: Simon & Schuster, First Touchstone Edition, 1995). This does not imply that a person should support or enable dysfunctional relationships, personal or organizational; Christians strive to correct such situations in accordance with scriptural guidance (i.e., 1 Cor 4:21; 2 Tim 4.2).

34 This is familiar hymnography in Orthodox liturgical practice as regards the Mother of God.

35 *Creation and Redemption*, "The Ever-Virgin Mother of God," 178; cf. St. Irenaeus of Lyons, especially his remarks about recapitulation, regeneration, and recirculation in *Adv. Haeres.* 3.18.1; 6.1.3; 3.22.4.

Vocation and Ethics

Stanley Samuel Harakas

Introduction

How might we understand "vocation" or "calling" from the specific perspective of Orthodox Christian ethics? To start with, it will be helpful to establish what is here meant by "vocation" from the perspective of Orthodox Christian theology, for the very topic could be questioned on the basis of traditional Orthodox theological teaching. Indeed, we must ask: Is the idea of "vocation" a proper and valid Orthodox Christian concept? Before discussing the important relationship between "vocation" and Orthodox Christian ethics, I will answer this question.

Let us first clarify our terminology. The word "vocation" comes from the Latin "*vocacio*," meaning "a summons" or a "strong inclination to a particular state or course of action, especially a divine call to the religious life." The word is based on the Latin term "*vox*," meaning "voice." [1] In contemporary English the term "vocation" has also come to mean an occupation by which an individual earns a living. In this sense our society speaks of "vocational education," "vocational training," and even "vocationalism" in educational theory. [2]

The word "call" has its roots in the Old Norse, Old

English, Old High German, and interestingly, in Old Church Slavonic. Its root meanings are "to call loudly," "to function as a battle herald," or simply to "talk loudly." Not mentioned is the Greek verb *"kalew,"* in spite of its obvious lectic similarity, having precisely the same meaning, that is, "to call," and in its passive form, "to be called."[3] Interestingly, the *Oxford English Dictionary* defines "vocation" by using "calling." Vocation is:

> the action on the part of God calling a person to exercise some special function, especially of a spiritual nature, or to fill a certain position; divine influence or guidance towards a definite (esp. religious) career, the fact of being so called or directed towards a special work in life; natural tendency to, or fitness for, such work.[4]

Indeed, it is clear that the very concepts of "vocation" and "calling" imply something more than the desire to be or to do something. It implies at least a "caller" and "the one who is called."

The Theological Appropriateness of the Concept of "Calling"

Calling in Scripture

The first question is whether it is appropriate from an Orthodox Christian perspective to speak of "calling," "callings," "vocation," or "vocations," at all. To answer this, we go first to the Old Testament, where one can discern many "callings" connected especially to the "prophetic calling." Moses at the burning bush is the first of three examples I wish to offer for our attention. The passage from Exodus reads as follows:

> Now Moses was keeping the flock of his father-in-law, Jethro, the priest of Midian; and he led his flock to the

west side of the wilderness, and came to Horeb, the mountain of God. And the angel of the Lord appeared to him in a flame of fire out of the midst of a bush; and he looked, and lo, the bush was burning, yet it was not consumed. And Moses said, "I will turn aside and see this great sight, why the bush is not burnt." When the Lord saw that he turned aside to see, God called to him out of the bush, "Moses, Moses!" And he said, "Here am I." (Exod 3:1-3)

The second passage describes the calling of the Prophet Isaiah: "And I heard the voice of the Lord saying, 'Whom shall I send, and who will go for us?' Then I said, 'Here am I! Send me'." (Isa 6:8)

The third and perhaps most dramatic is that of the young Prophet Samuel. While still a child, Samuel is called by God repeatedly, without response, until his mentor Eli tells him to acknowledge that he recognizes that it is God who is calling him.

Now the boy Samuel was ministering to the Lord under Eli. And the word of the Lord was rare in those days; there was no frequent vision. Yet, the lamp of God had not yet gone out, and Samuel was lying down within the temple of the Lord, where the ark of God was. Then the Lord called, "Samuel! Samuel!" and he said, "Here I am!" And the Lord called again, "Samuel!" And Samuel arose and went to Eli, and said, "Here I am, for you called me." But he said, "I did not call, my son; lie down again." Now Samuel did not yet know the Lord, and the word of the Lord had not yet been revealed to him. And the Lord called Samuel again the third time. And he arose and went to Eli, and said, "Here I am, for you called me." Then Eli perceived that the Lord was calling the boy. Therefore Eli said to Samuel, "Go, lie down; and if he calls you, you shall say, 'Speak, Lord, for thy servant hears.'" So Samuel went and lay down in his place.

> And the Lord came and stood forth, calling as at other
> times, "Samuel! Samuel!" And Samuel said, "Speak,
> for thy servant hears." Then the Lord said to Samuel,
> "Behold, I am about to do a thing in Israel, at which
> the two ears of everyone that hears it will tingle." (1
> Sam 3:1-11)

Clearly, in these three examples, for the "call" to be actually a "calling," two things are essential. First, that God calls, and secondly, that the one to whom the call is directed responds. The whole course of sacred history and even world history would have been different if Moses had walked away from the curious burning bush, or if Isaiah had responded to his vision with "Who cares!" or if Samuel had simply rolled over and gone on sleeping. God's call requires a conscious and willed response. Only then is a "calling" a "Calling." Vocation by definition is synergistic.

This becomes quite clear in the New Testament. On the one hand, the call by Jesus to his apostles and others is always cast in terms of a strong and compelling invitation, but not a compulsion. He says "follow me" to Peter and Andrew (Matt 4:19); to the inquirer who first wanted to bury his father (Matt 8:22, Luke 9:59); to Matthew (Matt 9:9, Mark 2:14, Luke 5:27); to Philip (John 1:43); to the disciples, with the promise that they would become "fishers of men" (Mark 1:17); and to the inquiring rich man, who in the end was unwilling to follow Jesus (Mark 10:21). We see the need for a personal response to the call in the frequent use of conditional phrases beginning with "If." For example, "Then Jesus told his disciples, 'If any man would come after me, let him deny himself and take up his cross and follow me'" (Matt 16:24).[5] The disciple is faced with the clear choice to follow Christ or not, and must respond.

The New Testament also expands the idea of "calling" to describe the summons to respond to the saving and redemptive work of Jesus Christ. Thus, the whole Christian life is understood as a calling to which the Christian responds. In the introduction to his first letter to the Corinthians, St. Paul speaks of this kind of calling: "Paul, called by the will of God to be an apostle of Christ Jesus, and our brother Sosthenes, To the church of God which is at Corinth, to those sanctified in Christ Jesus, called to be saints together with all those who in every place call on the name of our Lord Jesus Christ, both their Lord and ours" (1 Cor 1:1-2). Paul understands himself as called by God through his Damascus road experience. But he also identifies the members of the Corinthian Church as "called to be saints together with all those who in every place call on the name of our Lord Jesus Christ." The implication, of course, is that the Corinthian Christians may or may not respond positively to this call to be saints.

Another such passage is found in Ephesians, where we read about "the hope to which (God) has called (the Ephesian Christians)" and to "the riches of his glorious inheritance in the saints" (Eph 1:18). The assumption is that the "hope" will not be fulfilled without the affirmative and energetic response to the call by the Ephesian believers.

Then, in 2 Timothy we read of God "who saved us and called us with a holy calling, not in virtue of our works but in virtue of his own purpose and the grace which he gave us in Christ Jesus" (2 Tim 1:9). The early Church Father St. John Chrysostom comments on this passage:

> But how were they "called with a holy calling"? This

means, he made them saints, who were sinners and
enemies. "And this not of ourselves, it was the gift of
God." If then he is mighty in calling us, and good,
in that he hath done it of grace and not of debt, we
ought not to fear. For he who, when we should have
perished, saved us, though enemies, by grace, will he
not much more cooperate with us, when he sees us
working? "Not according to our own works," he says,
"but according to his own purpose and grace," that is,
no one compelling, no one counseling him, but of his
own purpose, from the impulse of his own goodness,
he saved us.[6]

Chrysostom emphasizes the volitional character of
the human response to God's initiative for a "holy calling," for he speaks of God cooperating with us! There
is a sense in which our own energetic response to God's
call, born out of our own free will, is an imitation of
God's good, un-compelled offer of salvation to us.

The Development of Calling and Vocation

Briefly I will mention the historical development of
the terms calling and vocation. A glance at the entry
"klesis" (with an *eta*) in Lampe's *Patristic Greek Lexicon*
shows frequent use of the term by numerous Church
fathers and ecclesial writers almost exclusively in the
sense of our calling as Christians and followers of
Christ. For example Justin Martyr speaks of "the calling of the new and eternal covenant, that is, the covenant of Christ."[7] That is the exclusive meaning of the
word *klesis* in the patristic corpus.

But what about "calling" and "vocation" in the ordinary occupations of life according to the Scriptures, or
the patristic corpus, or in the canons, the hymnology
and worship of the Orthodox Church? Historically,
you will not find much, if any, reference to such un-

derstandings of "calling." Rupert Davies notes clearly that in the biblical tradition, "There is no suggestion that God calls anyone to enter a particular profession or occupation," beyond the basic idea that Christians are "expected to show in daily life and that they are so called (as Christian persons)."[8]

Nevertheless, the concept of "vocation" was expanded in the West. Davies traces the reason for this development in two stages. First, there evolved a Western medieval distinction between "precepts," to be followed by those in the ordinary Christian life, and "counsels of perfection," something than only monastics could do. The next step was the rejection by Luther and Calvin of this "double standard." Davies writes, regarding Luther's position on 1Corinthians 7:7-24,

> he maintained that all stations in life in which it is possible to live honestly are divine vocations. They include those which are to be found in the family – to be husband, father, wife, mother – those which belong to economic and commercial life – to be cobbler, shopkeeper, milkmaid or slave – and those which are part of political life – to be king, governor or a soldier.[9]

This is seen as the historical beginning to speaking of an ordinary occupation in life as a divine vocation or calling from God.

Conclusions on Theological Appropriateness for Orthodox Christians

Given the early tradition of the Church in which "calling" is used to refer to the profound call to follow Christ, it is not common to Orthodox Christian thinking to speak of every job, every station in life, and every form of employment as in themselves callings from

God. Yet at the same time, it is clear from the scriptural passages above that every Christian by nature of his or her baptism is called by God to live fully and in accordance with the new life in Christ. So, can we legitimately speak of our various employments in the economic and social spheres, our roles as spouses and parents, the exercise of political authority, and so on, with theological accuracy, as "callings" or "vocations"?

I believe that it is hard to make the case that anyone who is a wife, an employer, an employee, a factory worker, a salesperson, and so on, precisely and exclusively because of that status or role has a specific calling from God to be that. Any modern secularist may function in those roles, but is it reasonable to say that God has called him or her to those roles? Further doubt is cast on such an understanding of ordinary endeavors by rapidly changing technology, political circumstances, economic fluidity in jobs and employment, to mention just a few of the changing characteristics of contemporary culture. Does God literally "call" the Third World physician to be a physician for a period of time, but then change this "call" when the physician flees a dictatorial government, and comes to the United States, only to find out that the best his Third World education can get him or her is a nurse's position? What if he or she then gives up on medicine and becomes a stockbroker? Is it reasonable to argue from the Christian positions outlined above that God is thus some kind of celestial employment agency? I think not.

Nevertheless, from the spiritual and ethical dimension, I believe that a strong case can be made not for the occupation or role itself, but for the way in which an Orthodox Christian approaches those roles and occupations. The basic "call" we have is to be fully human, growing in holiness so as to fulfill the image of God in us, precisely as a result of the restoration of the likeness of God in which we have been created by the redeeming and saving work of Jesus Christ. This fundamental Christian call to which we have been called is not exercised in a vacuum. It must always be incarnated in real experience.

This is clear from St. Paul's teaching in 1 Corinthians 7, where he applies the terminology of "calling" to Jews and Gentiles who become Christians. He refers to the issues of those who were circumcised as Jews, and those who were not, as Gentiles. For Paul, this distinction of circumcision has become insignificant.

> Let each one lead the life which the Lord has assigned to him, and in which God has called him. This is my rule in all the churches. Was anyone at the time of his call already circumcised? Let him not seek to remove the marks of circumcision. Was anyone at the time of his call uncircumcised? Let him not seek circumcision. (1 Cor 7:17-18)

The conclusion seems to imply an understanding of "calling" as something occurring apart from, perhaps in spite of, and without change in one's current situation in life. "Each one should remain in the state in which he was called" (v. 20). Yet regarding this perspective on one's current situation remaining static, this is challenged in the immediately following verse, when St. Paul speaks to slaves about their status. "Were you a slave when called? Never mind. But if you can gain your freedom, avail yourself of the opportunity" (1 Cor 7:21). How could St. Paul say that a person was "called" to be a slave by God, and yet concurrently urge the slave to "avail himself of the opportunity" to gain his freedom if he had the opportunity? The mistake here is in confusing being called *as* a slave and being called *when* a slave. The calling is irrespective of one's current situation/occupation. While Paul counsels generally that Christians are not to seek to change their status, here he also betrays an openness to improving or changing that very status!

While in general the call from God is not *as* or *to* a certain occupation or outward circumstance of life, this understanding is not without its grey areas. These make the question of speaking about callings or vocations in the common occupations or conditions of life not a black and white issue. In at least three specific circumstances, certain ordinary or common occupations can be considered "callings" in some fashion: the priesthood, monasticism or marriage, and the call to use our God-given gifts.

The Calling of the Priesthood

For decades at Holy Cross Greek Orthodox School of Theology, we have fostered a vocational approach with those who come to be educated and trained for the priesthood. We have already mentioned *"klesis,"* the call from God. This word is written with the Greek vowel *eta*, and can be used to speak of how men can be "called" by God to the priesthood. The calling follows the prior calling to the Christian life, and is indeed to be understood by many as a specific *calling to the priesthood*. St. Paul clearly understood his apostolic ministry as a calling. He declares in his letter to the Romans, "Paul, a servant of Jesus Christ, called to be an apostle, set apart for the gospel of God" (Rom 1:1). Elsewhere, he expresses his conviction of an almost eternal calling to his apostolic ministry, saying that God "had set me apart before I was born, and had called me through his grace" (Gal 1:15). In such a context, the words of St. Cyril of Alexandria, while commenting on the "I am the Good Shepherd" passage in John 10, have application. He says that "the ability to govern and lead flocks of people comes only through grace given from above, and not from ambitious endeavors."[10]

But our discussion with students about priestly vocations was not devoted exclusively to the divine call. It focused also on its antipode, the word *klisis,* a homonym, but written with the Greek letter *iota,* which is the root word for "inclination" or "personal talents, capacities, and abilities, including spiritual and moral proclivities." These are in part "gifts of the Holy Spirit," and in part, the natural and diverse proclivities in all human beings. In the life of the Church, they are the capacities of the various members of the Body of Christ as discussed by St. Paul in 1 Corinthians, chapter 12, where he writes: "Now there are varieties of gifts, but the same Spirit; and there are varieties of service, but the same Lord; and there are varieties of working, but it is the same God who inspires them all in everyone. To each is given the manifestation of the Spirit for the common good" (1 Cor 12:4-7). These "varieties" are primarily spoken of in reference to the life of the Church, but in this case, these gifts spread out into all of life, as well as where Christians live, working out their salvation (Phil 2:12).

As administrators and faculty, charged with the spiritual development of our student candidates to the priestly service, it was part of our task to discern with God's help whether indeed a student had both the calling (*klesis* with an *eta*) and the capacities, desire, and abilities (*klisis* with a *iota*). There were times when we had to counsel a candidate that he was lacking in either the first or the second, or both.

The Call to Celibacy or Marriage

Another grey area is the call to the celibate life and the call to the married life. Here we have an interesting distinction in the Christian calling in general. It was Jesus, as described in the Gospel of Matthew, who, when answering a question about divorce, articulated the issue.

> And Pharisees came up to him and tested him by asking, "Is it lawful to divorce one's wife for any cause?" He answered, "Have you not read that he who made them from the beginning made them male and female, and said, 'For this reason a man shall leave his father and mother and be joined to his wife, and the two shall become one flesh'? So they are no longer two but one flesh. What therefore God has joined together, let not man put asunder." They said to him, "Why then did Moses command one to give a certificate of divorce, and to put her away?"
> He said to them, "For your hardness of heart Moses allowed you to divorce your wives, but from the beginning it was not so. And I say to you: whoever divorces his wife, except for unchastity, and marries another, commits adultery."
> The disciples said to him, "If such is the case of a man with his wife, it is not expedient to marry." But he said to them, "Not all men can receive this saying, but only those to whom it is given. For there are eunuchs who have been so from birth, and there are eunuchs who have been made eunuchs by men, and there are eunuchs who have made themselves eunuchs for the sake of the kingdom of heaven. He who is able to receive this, let him receive it." (Matt 19:2-12)

Marriage is clearly seen as a relationship and institution given by God, and in principle not to be terminated by divorce. Regarding the term "eunuch," the patristic texts unanimously see it as referring to the exceptional behavior of avoidance of marriage and sexual relationships in it or outside of it. Equally consistent is the emphasis on the lack of virtue in the two first cases of being born without sexual interests or being forcibly deprived of them. The third alternative is universally praised as an act of volition, a choice for celibacy made for the sake of the kingdom of heaven. Thus, St. Jerome says:

> "The last group are promised the reward. The other two, for whom chastity is not a matter of willing but necessity, are due nothing at all . . . Only the person who for Christ seeks chastity wholeheartedly and cuts off sexual impurity altogether [is the genuine eunuch]. So he adds, "He who is able to receive this, let him receive it," so that each of us should look to his own strength as to whether he can carry out the commands of virginity and chastity."[11]

Yet, in Christ's explanation from the Gospel of Matthew above, the implication is made that virginity and chastity is somehow a calling in the sense that it is a subjective ability to hear such an invitation and to respond to it voluntarily; the phrases "Not all men can receive this saying, but only those to whom it is given," and "He who is able to receive this, let him receive it" imply the existence of an invitation to the virginal life that comes both from outside the person and from within. Here, while the terminology of "call" is not explicitly applied to the marital or celibate life, the inclination (perhaps even the "drive") toward either the one or the other is acknowledged.

Commenting on Matthew's passage, Euthymios Zigabenos, the twelfth-century Byzantine biblical commentator, describes it not as a calling but as a gift: "Only those can accept and maintain this word, to whom this gift has been given by God (*dedotai touto to dwron para Theou*)."[12] In either case the willing response is highlighted in the patristic understanding; when speaking of "gift" or of "call," the emphasis is on the decision of the individual to respond. Chrysostom emphasizes that "God does not leave the conclusion to the requirements of the law"; Zigabenos summarizes: "(Jesus) leaves the issue to the choice of persons."[13]

The Call to Use our God-given Gifts

Finally, it may be affirmed that there is evidence for something less intense than the kind of "call" St. Paul received on the way to Damascus, but also something more than just the prudential choosing of a career on the basis of accidents of time, place and circumstance. I am pointing to the talents that are inherent in all persons, which the Christian sees as "gifts," for the upbuilding of the Church and the enriching of the common good.

The call to use the talents and gifts granted to us is found in Jesus' parable of the talents (Matt 25:14-30; Luke 19:11:28). Of the many interpretations of the meaning of the "talents" given, St. Cyril of Alexandria comes closest to our interests here. He speaks of the recipients of the talents as "to each giving a spiritual gift so that he [or she] might have character and aptitude." As a result, those who receive these talents are "fit to carry out the work of God." Regarding the recipient of the one talent who buried it, Cyril says, "He kept the gift hidden, making it unprofitable for others and useless for himself . . . The Spirit and the gift of the divine gifts have departed from such as these."[14] We are reminded here of St. Paul's words to the Christians of Galatia: "You were called to freedom, brethren; only do not use your freedom as an opportunity for the flesh, but through love be servants of one another" (Gal.5:13). "Talents" in this sense are not a specific calling, but specific gifts we are given by God, which we as persons who have received the call of the new life in Christ are responsible to cultivate.

This notion is further supported by the passage in Romans: "We know that in everything God works for good with those who love him, who are called according to his purpose" (Rom 8:28). "Everything" certainly includes the way that persons earn their livings, even as in our contemporary society one's type of employment can shift over the years. So also, in 2 Peter, we read that "(God's) divine power has granted to us all things that pertain to life and godliness, through the knowledge of him who called us to his own glory and excellence" (2 Pet 1:3). "All things," can surely be understood as including the normal daily commitments and activities of life. The same can also be understood from St. Paul's exhortation to the Christians of Ephesus, when he said, "I therefore, a prisoner for the Lord, beg you to lead a life worthy of the calling to which you have been called" (Eph 4:1).

In Sum

The conclusion is that our "calling" or "vocation" is, at its core, a call to the life in Christ. "Leading a life worthy of the calling," is a matter of functioning as a Christian in whatever circumstances or situation we are embedded. For example, the specifics into which our talents and gifts have led us, whether we be clergy or laity, married or celibate, citizen or political leader, wealthy or poor; the work we do, the family of which we are part, the relaxation and entertainment we allow to ourselves; the friends we keep, and so on – these are all the specific venues in which we are to exercise our callings worthily and not unworthily, responsibly and not irresponsibly, conscientiously and not with disregard, for the benefit of the Church and others, and our own spiritual growth, and not selfishly or in self-absorption with ourselves.

If we want to refer to these situations as "callings," implying a combination of choices, abilities and talents, as gifts from God, it seems to me that the Christian may do so. But often it is unclear whether reference to "calling" or "vocation" has become just another secular term for what we determine are our desires. As Rupert Davies observes, in large measure in modern times "the religious element has been drained out of the concept, and everyone regards himself as entitled to speak of his calling without any reference to God."[15]

I recently came across evidence of this secular use of "vocation" on the wall of a local Wendy's restaurant where I live. The following sign was posted, entitled "A Boy with a Plan":

> "My vocation has to do with restaurants" could be considered an understatement from the creator of a multi-billion-dollar restaurant empire, but when Dave Thomas wrote these words in 1948, he was a 16-year-old student at Central High School in Fort Wayne, Indiana. Here is a simple philosophy of hard work and perseverance upon which Wendy's was founded. This is a remarkable document from a boy who knew what he wanted and how to get it.[16]

It is likely that the word "vocation" came into Dave Thomas' vocabulary from some religious source; I have not researched it. But it is doubtful, on the basis of any Orthodox criteria, that God specifically called the young man to establish a chain of restaurants. No mention in the statement is made of such a divine dimension regarding the establishment of his business. "Hard work" and "perseverance" are the terms that give substance to the use of "vocation," but these not exclusively virtues of Christians.

From the perspective on vocation I have been outlining above, I would argue that the issue is not so much that as a young person Thomas was committed to a career in the restaurant business. The issue rather is how he acted, how he was motivated, how he dealt with employers and customers, and if these kinds of things were in fact expressions of a spiritual and specifically Christian understanding of his calling to the life in Christ.

What we recognize here is that this formulation of the topic of "calling" or "vocation" is by definition an ethical issue: it deals with values, choices, decisions and commitments.

Calling / Vocation and Ethics

An Eastern Orthodox Approach to Ethics

By the term "ethics" I mean what is dealt with by "normative language," that is, language that establishes the norm for right human behavior. Whenever we use or imply words such as "ought," "ought not," "should," "should not," "thou shalt," "thou shalt not," or language that implies praise or blame through emotive statements, we are using "normative language."

Ethics also includes decision-making processes.

For the Orthodox Church, these are all rooted in the doctrinal, canonical, worship, ascetical, pastoral "Tradition and traditions" of the Orthodox faith. Orthodox ethics discusses the norms and standards of Christian life by drawing on the faith tradition of the early undivided Church and what the Church understands as values and disvalues, virtues and vices, and theological truths as contrasted to theological denials or distortions of the Christian faith. [17]

What follows is a recent effort to develop an Orthodox Christian ethical approach on another topic, but equally effective, I believe, to address the issue of vocation and ethics.[18] This approach of Orthodox ethics is applicable to many different areas of modern concern which range from the concerns regarding liturgy[19] to bioethics[20] to stewardship[21] and to many other topics.[22] So also, in this discussion of "vocation" or "calling" I seek to flesh out what I believe to be an authentic understanding and conceptualization of Orthodox Christian ethics.

To say that the Eastern Orthodox Christian approach to ethics is based on the theological presuppositions of the Orthodox faith is to assert the following: The Trinitarian God is the Good, and as such God is the source of all Good in human experience. Human beings are created in the image and likeness of the Good God, but as a result of ancestral and personal sin, all human beings exist in a condition of brokenness and separation from the source of the Good, who is God. The condition of spiritual and moral brokenness means that our human condition makes us incapable of realizing the fullness of goodness personally, in interpersonal relationships, or as societies. Our perception of right and wrong, good and evil, the fitting and unfitting, is darkened, our wills are distorted, and our intentions and motivations are confused and garbled.

Nevertheless, we are not irreducibly evil. There remain in human life, in weakened form, many moral capacities, such as the sense of the moral and a striving for ethical understanding, a self-determining capacity to choose good over evil, the ability to conform one's life to Godlikeness in many circumstances, and to do what approximates the Good. In short, the empirical human condition allows us to choose to do at least a modicum of good and occasionally to flash brightly as ethical beings – but achieving the fullness of goodness is beyond us in our fallen condition.

In the redemptive work of Jesus Christ, however, the potential for full human Godlike existence is restored. From the ethical perspective the Christian life consists of an ongoing, life-long, never-ending, grace-empowered process of growth toward the fulfillment of the divine image in each human being. Thus, the ethical and moral life is a process, requiring on the human side struggle to overcome evil and continuous effort to realize the good. However, this can take place in any measure of fullness only in communion with the Living God. While a low-level ethic allowing for the rudiments of human social living is accessible in some way to all human beings, realizing even a measure of Godlikeness in human life requires the ongoing, continuous presence of God in our lives. The doorkeeper of that living presence in most cases is faith in God, and in particular, in the Divine-Human Person and the saving work of Jesus Christ. It requires the willing acceptance, or renewal through constant repentance, of the presence of God in our lives as a normative guide to living. The oft-repeated Orthodox liturgical call, "Let us commit ourselves and one another and our whole life to Christ our God," normatively calls each Christian repeatedly to a reorientation of life. It is an evocative call, which is fundamentally an ethical imperative.

Thus, for Orthodox Christianity, virtues and vices, commandments and violations of commandments, morally fitting behaviors and inner dispositions, and their opposites, are understood in a theological context. Orthodox ethics is foundationally theological and spiritual.

Ethics and Vocation

From this perspective, the ethical and the vocational are integrally related. The experience of being called to a vocation through God's gifts to us, and responding to that call as seen in the historical Christian Church on the one hand, and the requirements of the moral life, on the other, demonstrate a connection between them, even though they can also be understood as separate spheres of experience.

In my book *Living the Faith: The* Praxis *of Eastern Orthodox Ethics*[23] an ethical approach to work and occupation is discussed. The text does not cast it in categories of "calling" or "vocation," but in the category of "mission in the service to others." Nonetheless, the ethical dimension to work and occupation is articulated in the spirit of what has been said above, regarding "calling" or "vocation" in reference to the exercise of many roles and functions of the Christian who perceives him or herself as "called" by God to a new way of living as a result of the new life in Christ.

Christian ethics respects all honest work and

perceives it as an ethical and appropriate contribution to the general well-being. Every worker should feel the dignity of work at the task that he or she does. Yet there are improper and unethical forms of work, such as those of the thief, the procurer of prostitutes, begging (as a profession), gambling in all its forms, illegal narcotic distribution, etc. Persons who have independent incomes, who do not have to be employed in order to maintain their lives, also have the responsibility to work. Such persons should work for the public welfare.

We have a moral responsibility to make appropriate and fitting choices regarding our employment. *Career choices* ought to be made in the light of our abilities, opportunities, education, interests, and obligation to be of service to our fellows, and, through them, to God. It is appropriate to seek education and training for the work or profession chosen. Every work or profession chosen should be perceived as a mission in which we cooperate with God in fulfilling the needs of His people and His world.[24]

This is an ethical approach for the Christian applicable to all aspects of life, in the light of the true calling the Christian is assumed to have by participating in the saving and redemptive work of Jesus Christ and as a member of the Church. As we have seen above, the "calling" to redemptive living in Christ pertains to "the gifts we have been given," "freedom," "all things that pertain to this life," and inclusively, "everything."

To receive and respond to a calling is to stand in the presence of the living God with awe and reverence, to praise, to pray, to glorify the Triune God. It is also to stand in the presence of the living God to receive grace,

blessings, forgiveness, strength, renewal and to experience the joy of the restoration of communion with God.
Both allow for the believer to experience growth in the
image and likeness of God personally, and to have a
foretaste of the communal life of the kingdom of God,
now and eschatologically.

However, this takes place neither automatically nor
magically. The process of growing toward Godlikeness
is understood in Eastern Orthodox ethics as synergistic. *Synergeia* toward rejecting evil and doing the good
as part of growing in the divine image is cooperation
between the living presence and power of God and the
thinking, willing, desiring and active effort of human
beings. The good is accomplished by human beings
only in conscious or unconscious *synergeia* with God's
divine energies. Orthodox theology identifies with
God's graceful presence. Thus communion with God
is the source of all that is good. The rejection of God is
the ultimate source of all evil.

For Orthodox Christian ethics, the empirical sources
for ethical reflection are found in all the revelatory expressions of God in the life of the Church. This doesn't
exclude philosophical or scientific or quasi-scientif-
ic reflection, but of much greater importance are the
Holy Scriptures, Holy Tradition, the Church Fathers
and Mothers, canon law, ascetic experience, the liturgical worship of the Church and, significantly for this
study, an analysis and understanding of the experience
of receiving a "vocation" or "calling" in the way one is
to live one's life as a Christian.

Orthodox Christian ethics, as a study of the normative dimension of human life, can analyze the ideas and
concepts of "vocation" or "calling" to identify the way
moral concerns are central to its various dimensions.

Ethical Requirements as Central to any Calling or Vocation

The ethics of calling or vocation focuses not on how a "calling," however understood, was accepted, but on how it is accomplished. Once there is the call to the Christian life, we must recognize immediately that exercising these callings is not something automatically understood or done. One thinks of the criticisms and corrections of St. Paul to the errant Christians of Corinth, and to the significant passages of the corpus of holy canons which seek to label, condemn, and correct behaviors which are contradictory to the values and lifestyle of the Christian way of life.

Living in accordance with the calling requires the growing application of love for the benefit of those entrusted to those who minister as a result of their calling. Jesus describes Himself as the Good Shepherd, saying "I am the good shepherd." And immediately He defines what He means: "The good shepherd lays down his life for the sheep" (John 10:11). For all who understand their lives as a response to God's call, they will live a moral and ethical life as part of the sacrificial love for the neighbor. This is primary ethical requirement as a positive response to God's call.

Ethical Requirements for the Vocation of Church Leadership

If Christ is the model for all Christians, then in particular he is the model for all those in the various ministries of the Church, and particularly the clergy. The clergyman sets the norms for pastoral service of the flock in a sacrificial manner. Thus, the priest must love and care for the "logical flock" of the body of Christ entrusted to him by the Church. He is to cultivate and possess the basic Christian virtues, and also those virtues that are essential for the exercise of his pastoral care of the faithful.

This is clearly illustrated by a biblical example from I Timothy that describes the ethical requirements of a bishop or priest.[25] The passage mixes both the positive traits and actions of a bishop that "ought" to be followed, with negative traits and behaviors that the bishop "ought not" have and do. Here, character traits and behaviors are either enjoined or condemned as ethical precepts. We read:

> The saying is sure: If anyone aspires to the office of bishop, he desires a noble task ... Now a bishop must be above reproach, the husband of one wife, temperate, sensible, dignified, hospitable, an apt teacher, no drunkard, not violent but gentle, not quarrelsome, and no lover of money. He must manage his own household well, keeping his children submissive and respectful in every way; for if a man does not know how to manage his own household, how can he care for God's church? He must not be a recent convert, or he may be puffed up with conceit and fall into the condemnation of the devil; moreover he must be well thought of by outsiders, or he may fall into reproach and the snare of the devil. (1 Tim 3:1-7)

In the light of the first part of this paper, we should observe that in the first lines of this passage from 1 Timothy there is no intimation about a divine from above "call" from God for anyone to become a bishop. There is no *klesis* (with an *eta*) here. There is, however, a *klisis* (with a *iota*) with the subjective aspect to it – "If anyone aspires to the office of bishop. . ."

But, it is equally important to note that the Greek verb for "aspires" is very strong – *oregetai* – which literally means to "stretch oneself out," and figuratively, to have an intense hunger for something. Also, the verb "desires" in the Greek text is equally strong – *epithy-*

mei – meaning literally, "to set one's heart upon" something.[26] Such strong aspirations and desires may well be a gift of the Spirit, to which, however, the passage does not give outright endorsement. It only affirms that the task is a noble one.

Perhaps the reason for this is that, ethically speaking, the requirements are quite demanding. Such a candidate is to be morally "above reproach," never divorced, "temperate," "sensible," "dignified," "hospitable," "gentle in character," "an apt teacher," a good husband and father of his children, an effective administrator, one who deeply cares for the Church and congregation entrusted to him, and who has a good reputation among those outside of the Church. This is a rather daunting list of ethical characteristics, and behaviors that the first-century bishop was called upon to fulfill.

In addition, there are a series of "ought nots." He is to be "no drunkard," not a person who acts violently, who cannot control his temper, nor a person who is argumentative, nor one who is motivated by greed. Further, he should not be new to the faith, with its likely concurrent vices of conceit, pride and inexperience so as to easily fall before temptations. We understand these ethical requirements to be so strict because the clergyman will be the overseer of the spiritual health of a community. He must model the sacrificial love of the neighbor. If he is caught up in his own vices, this becomes impossible.

The passage from 1 Timothy is one of several such lists of character traits and behaviors in the Scriptures[27] and in the subsequent literature of the Church, such as St. John Chrysostom's treatise *On the Priesthood*. Throughout the centuries, the canons of the Church and the wisdom of some of the spiritual lights have contributed to the literature about the "calling" of the clergyman. Integral to the calling or vocation of a church leader are the ethical norms that must precede the calling and be maintained throughout life.[28]

Ethical Requirements for the Vocation of the Laity

Ethical "oughts" and "ought nots" are also relevant for the laity of the Church. In the first case, and on the most elementary level, laypersons are also encouraged to aspire to "noble callings" in that every Christian is expected to grow spiritually and morally in the image and likeness of God, toward Godlikeness. It was not to clergy only, for instance, that the words "You, therefore, must be perfect, as your heavenly Father is perfect" (Matt 5:48) were addressed. There are many scriptural passages prescribing general behaviors to be followed by all Christians in all kinds of situations.[29] Thus, Romans 12:2 instructs generally: "Do not be conformed to this world but be transformed by the renewal of your mind, that you may prove what is the will of God, what is good and acceptable and perfect." A bit later in the Epistle to the Romans we hear of specific "oughts" and "ought nots" relevant for every Christian – clergy, monastic, or layperson:

> Owe no one anything, except to love one another; for he who loves his neighbor has fulfilled the law. The commandments, "You shall not commit adultery, You shall not kill, You shall not steal, You shall not covet," and any other commandment, are summed up in this sentence, "You shall love your neighbor as yourself." Love does no wrong to a neighbor; therefore love is the fulfilling of the law. (Rom 13:8-10)

From the general ethical "oughts" and "ought nots"

for every "vocation" or "calling", it is our work to determine more specific ethical imperatives. This is not the place to try to sketch out the specific ethical requirements of spouses, children, teachers, employees, employers, political officials, government employees, scientists, social workers, police, military personnel, and the myriads of occupations which are legitimately and appropriately exercised by the Christian. I have made an effort to sketch out the highlights of such occupational ethics in my book *Living the Faith: The* Praxis *of Eastern Orthodox Ethics.*[30]

However, by way of example of the kind of specificity that is possible and necessary, however, I will share the kind of concrete application of ethical values that is possible for a specific occupational realm. Professor Arlene H. Rinaldi of Florida Atlantic University has set up a site on the Internet to discuss the ethical guidelines for computer usage. She calls it "The Net: User Guidelines and Netiquette," and on this site she lists "The Ten Commandments for Computer Ethics," which she attributes to The Computer Ethics Institute.[31] This is her application for use in the contemporary world:

The Ten Commandments of Computer Use

1. Thou shalt not use a computer to harm other people.
2. Thou shalt not interfere with other people's computer work.
3. Thou shalt not snoop around in other people's files.
4. Thou shalt not use a computer to steal.
5. Thou shalt not use a computer to bear false witness.
6. Thou shalt not use or copy software for which you have not paid.
7. Thou shalt not use other people's computer resources without authorization.

8. Thou shalt not appropriate other people's intellectual output.

9. Thou shalt think about the social consequences of the program you write.

10. Thou shalt use a computer in ways that show consideration and respect.

It would not be hard to articulate similar "commandments" for the other spheres of contemporary life. For example, her Internet commandment, "Thou shalt think about the social consequences of the program you write," could be easily transformed into guidelines for the social responsibilities of businesses in their support of programs of public benefit.

The Call to Integrity

One last piece of the ethical dimension of vocation should be mentioned in closing. An ethical approach to vocation needs to be firmly integrated with virtue and character, with the moral and spiritual integrity of each person.

My Greek-English dictionary uses two words to provide the equivalent of the English word "integrity." And both of them are highly instructive. In the classical Greek language, the first word is *akeraios*, It was used by ancient Greek writers to express meanings such as "pure," "unmixed," "uncontaminated," "guileless," "incorruptible," "without reservation." Church Fathers used the word to mean, in addition, "soundness," "simplicity," and "innocence." A second Greek word for integrity is *olokleros*, pointing in classical Greek to "wholeness," or "completeness." Among the Church Fathers, the word came to mean "whole," "healthy," and "perfect" and is a synonym for the word *swos*, which is the root word for the word *swteria* meaning "salvation."

Integrity is at the heart of Jesus' teaching in the Sermon on the Mount (Matt 5-7). There, Jesus affirms the Old Testament Commandments but insists that the mere external appearance of following them is not good enough. He is concerned that the inner person, with his or her dispositions, motives and intents be in harmony with the external moral requirements. He is calling for spiritual and moral integrity.

In the wake of the 1990s business climate of "Greed is good," that led corporate executives to trade integrity for deceit, dishonesty and self-serving greed, the message is clear. Integrity of character is an essential aspect of human being and living. Everyone, no matter what his or her occupation, is called to be a person of integrity – not to appear to be one thing, and deliberately violate it. I believe that, if modern society in all of its dimensions wants to survive, prudence requires that it begin teaching in every dimension of its existence this basic morality and the integrity of character that empowers it.

Or perhaps I should say it must be reclaimed. What if Orthodox Christians took more seriously their responsibility to conduct their daily activities with the sense of having a "vocation" or "calling" to serve God and the public? For they would see something that others, without that sense, could not conceive, that indeed,

> he who loves his neighbor has fulfilled the law. The commandments, "You shall not commit adultery, You shall not kill, You shall not steal, You shall not covet," and any other commandment, are summed up in this sentence, "You shall love your neighbor as yourself." Love does no wrong to a neighbor; therefore love is the fulfilling of the law. (Rom 13:8-10)

Conclusion

In this contribution to the ongoing discussion of "vo-cation" I have argued that except for very few circum-stances, the terms "vocation" and "calling" should be applied to the gifts given to each person. Like the call-ing itself, these gifts are accepted voluntarily and lived out as gifts from God with integrity and wholeness of character in Christian commitment. Specifically, I have argued that the ethical imperative of the "call" to the Christian life is the overarching value that guides and directs the "oughts" and "ought nots" of the ethical ap-proach to our "vocations" and "callings" in the ordi-nary spheres of life.

Pronouncements of marital relations, professional codes of behavior, privacy regulations, the detailed specifics of industries and the like are important, but of little use if there is no adoption and implementa-tion of personal, ecclesial, corporate or governmental integrity. For the Christian person in any "vocation" or "calling," the most important consideration is to "lead a life worthy of the calling to which you have been called" (Eph 4:1).

Notes

1 *Merriam-Webster's Collegiate Dictionary – Tenth Ed.* Springfield, MA: Merriam-Webster International, 1996, 1323.
2 See for example Bettina A. Lankard, "SCANS and the New Vo-cationalism" at http://www.ericdigests.org/1996-3/scans.htm ; James D. Marshall, "Dewey and the new 'Vocationalism'" http://www.ed.uiuc.edu/EPS/PES-yearbook/97_docs/marshall.html ; Terry Hyland, "Vocationalism, Work, and the Future of Higher Education." *Journal of Vocational Education and Training* 53, no. 4 (2001).
3 Between the two words, "vocation" and "calling," I prefer the

latter precisely because the term "vocation" has an overload of reduced meanings in English, from the Latin, such as "vocations" understood for years in Western society as limited to the priestly calling. Nevertheless, I use both in this paper.

4 Quoted by Mary Ann Donovan, S.C., "The Vocation of the Theologian." *Theological Studies,* March, 2004, vol. 65, no. 1, 4.

5 See also Matthew 16:24 –"Then Jesus told his disciples, 'If any man would come after me, let him deny himself and take up his cross and follow me;" Matthew 19:21 – "Jesus said to him, 'If you would be perfect, go, sell what you possess and give to the poor, and you will have treasure in heaven; and come, follow me;'" Mark 8:34, Luke 9:23 – "And he called to him the multitude with his disciples, and said to them, 'If any man would come after me, let him deny himself and take up his cross and follow me;'" and John 12:26 – "If anyone serves me, he must follow me; and where I am, there shall my servant be also; if anyone serves me, the Father will honor him."

6 *On 2 Timothy*, Homily 2, 1:9 Nicene and Post-Nicene Fathers, series I, vol. XIII.

7 *Dialogue With Trypho*, 118, 3. Migne 6, 749c. In G.W.H. Lampe, *A Patristic Greek Lexicon*, Oxford: Clarendon Press, 1968, 757-758. In contemporary theology, the concept of "covenant" is also being expanded, to the detriment of the original biblical concept of "covenant" as part of God's redemptive plan for the salvation of humanity and the world, such as the concept of covenant applied to marriage and to political and other secular concerns. I don't believe that it is possible to find any warrants for this expansion in the biblical and patristic tradition.

8 "Vocation" in *The Westminster Dictionary of Christian Theology.* Philadelphia: The Westminster Press, 1983. Ed. Alan Richardson and John Bowden, 601.

9 Ibid., 601-602. Davies actually begins by saying that Luther's interpretation of 1 Cor 7.7-24 is "now considered false..."

10 *Commentary on the Gospel According to St. John.* Library of the Fathers of the Holy Catholic Church, Anterior to the Division of East and West. London: Walter Smith, 1885, vol. II, book 6, 1, 67.

11 *Commentary on Matthew 3.19.12* in *Corpus Christianorum. Series Latina* 77:168-169, quoted in *Ancient Christian Commentary on Scripture: New Testament. Matthew 14-28. Vol. 1b.* Downers Grove:

InterVarsity Press, 2002, 94.

12 Quoted in Panagiotes Trembelas, *Hypomnema eis ton Kata Ioannen Evaggelion,* Athens: "Zoe" Publications, 1951, 359.

13 Ibid., 360.

14 *Fragment 283. Mattthaus-Kommentare aus der greichischen Kirche.* Ed. Joseph Reuss. Berlin: Akademie-Verlag, 1957.Quoted in *Ancient Christian Commentary on Scripture,* op. cit., 222.

15 "Vocation," op. cit., 602

16 Wendy's Restaurant, 14339 Spring Hill Drive, Spring Hill, FL. April, 2004.

17 See Harakas, *Toward Transfigured Life: The "Theoria" of Eastern Orthodox Ethics.*

18 This is an account of Orthodox Christian ethics, as offered in my article "Ethics and Stewardship," modified significantly to adapt it to the issue of vocation.

19 Ibid.

20 Stanley S. Harakas, *For the Health of Body and Soul: An Eastern Orthodox Introduction to Bioethics.* Brookline: Holy Cross Orthodox Press, 1980. _____, *Health and Medicine in the Eastern Orthodox Tradition.* New York: Crossroad, 1990. Second printing – Minneapolis: Light and Life Publishing Co., 1996. John Breck, *The Sacred Gift of Life: Orthodox Chrisitanity and Bioethics.* Crestwood, NY: St. Vladimir's Seminary Press, 2000.

21 Stanley S. Harakas, "Ethics and Stewardship" in *Good and Faithful Servant: Stewardship in the Orthodox Church.* Ed. Anthony Scott. Crestwood, NY: St. Vladimir's Seminary Press, 2003, ch. 10.

22 Stanley S. Harakas, *Contemporary Moral Issues Facing the Orthodox Christian.* Minneapolis: Light and Life Publishing Co, 1982. John Breck, *God with Us: Critical Issues in Christian Life and Faith.* Crestwood, NY: St. Vladimir's Seminary Press, 2003. Bishop's Council of the Russian Orthodox Church, *The Orthodox Church and Society: The Basis of the Social Concept of the Russian Orthodox Church.* Belleville, MI: St. Innocent/Firebird Publishers, 2000.

23 Minneapolis: Light and Life, 1992.

24 Ibid., 150.

25 In the early Church, the bishop functioned in the same way as the modern-day priest.

26 Fritz Rienecker, *A Linquistic Key to the Greek New Testament.* Grand Rapids: Zondervan Publishing House, 1982, 622.

27 For example, Titus 1:7-9: "For a bishop, as God's steward, must be blameless; he must not be arrogant or quick-tempered or a drunkard or violent or greedy for gain, but hospitable, a lover of goodness, master of himself, upright, holy, and self-controlled; he must hold firm to the sure word as taught, so that he may be able to give instruction in sound doctrine and also to confute those who contradict it."

28 Each age seems to have it own particular vice that falls upon some of the clergy. In our own times it is clergy sexual misconduct. So, in a way never before seen in the history of the Church, the "oughts" and "ought nots" concerning this aspect of the priestly ministry are being studied, developed and promulgated as guidelines and directives for clergy behavior. The Greek Orthodox Archdiocese has already issued a set of such guidelines, available on the Internet at http://www.goarch.org/goa/documents/misconduct_policy.asp. In addition, at this writing a special committee of the Standing Conference of the Canonical Orthodox Bishops in America (SCOBA) is working on a policy regarding this important issue that will eventually be implemented among and within all canonical Orthodox Churches in America.

29 Ethicists call this the "middle axiom" level.

30 Minneapolis: Light and Life Publishing Co. 1992.

31 (http://www.fau.edu/netiquette/net/ten.html)

The Priesthood of the Laity

PAUL MEYENDORFF

> …You are a chosen race, a royal priesthood, a holy
> nation, God's own people, that you may declare
> the wonderful deeds of him who called you out of
> darkness into his marvelous light. (1 Pet 2:9)

With these words, the author of the epistle seeks to
encourage the Christians of Asia Minor while they
face persecution. In their suffering they are to imitate
Christ. They are to imitate him also in the proclamation of the gospel, the good news, to the world. In this
way, they are to share in the priestly ministry of Christ
himself.

In our day, however, Orthodox Christians have largely
forgotten the notion that the laity,[1] the people of God, is
a royal priesthood. When we consider the meaning of
priesthood, we think immediately of ordained clergy,
bishops and priests. Yet in the New Testament the term
priest (in Greek: *hiereus*) is never used for ordained clergy, but either for Christ, who is the one "high priest,"[2]
or for all the faithful baptized:

> Come to him, to that living stone, rejected by men but
> in God's sight chosen and precious; and like living
> stones be yourselves built into a spiritual house, to be
> a *holy priesthood*, to offer spiritual sacrifices acceptable
> to God through Jesus Christ. (1 Pet 2:5)

Only in later centuries was the notion of priesthood attached to ordained ministry. With this development, however, the priesthood of the laity, of all the baptized, came to be neglected, if not entirely forgotten.[3] Yet, through Christian baptism, through our incorporation into the Body of Christ,[4] we become sharers also in his priestly ministry.

Let us examine, therefore, the implications of our common priesthood. We will do this in three steps. First, we should understand the meaning of priesthood. Second, we shall see how this priesthood of all the faithful is expressed in the liturgy.[5] Third, we shall look at the implications of this for our life as Christians today.

Priesthood

In pagan antiquity, priests were understood to be intermediaries between the gods and humanity. Their primary task was to offer sacrifices to the gods on behalf of the people. Thus they typically performed their functions in temples, which were understood as the dwelling-place of the gods. The sacrifices they offered were intended both to placate the gods and to seek divine favor. They also interpreted the divine oracles, thus revealing the divine will to humans.

In the Old Testament, the priesthood was practiced in several ways.[6] In the early period of Israel's history, patriarchs fulfilled the role.[7] Later on, the priesthood passed to the tribe of Levi (and was thus referred to as "Levitical priesthood"), and the task became professionalized. A king in the Old Testament exercised a priestly function, such as the warrior-king Melchizedek,[8] who is mentioned in the psalms as a messianic figure: "You

are a priest forever after the order of Melchizedek."[9]
Not surprisingly, this model of priesthood is applied to
Jesus Christ in the New Testament, specifically in the
Epistle to the Hebrews.[10]

During these periods, priests performed functions similar to those of pagan priests, as we see
from the description of their functions in the book of
Deuteronomy:

> And of Levi he said, "Give to Levi your Thummim
> and your Urim to your godly one, whom you did test
> at Massah, with whom you did strive at the waters of
> Meribah; who said of his father and mother, 'I regard
> them not'; he disowned his brothers and ignored his
> children. For they observed your word and kept your
> covenant. They shall teach Jacob your ordinances, and
> Israel your law; they shall put incense before you, and
> whole burnt offerings upon your altar.[11]

These Levitical priests consulted the *Urim* and
Thummim, the sacred lots which were used to provide
answers to questions posed to God.[12] They taught and
interpreted the law, the Torah, to the people. And they
performed sacrifices and cultic offerings.

In the later period of the Old Testament, the first
two of these functions passed to the prophets and the
scribes, and the essential function of the priesthood was
reduced to the offering of sacrifice. This is reflected in a
passage such as Heb 5:1: "For every high priest chosen
from among men is appointed to act on behalf of men
in relation to God, to offer gifts and sacrifices for sins."
In Judaism, as in pagan antiquity, priests functioned as
mediators between God and humanity – and this is precisely how Christ is presented in the New Testament,
particularly in the Epistle to the Hebrews.[13]

The Priesthood of Christ
in the Epistle to the Hebrews

The Epistle to the Hebrews is the only New Testament book to concentrate on the notion of priesthood, so it is here this study focuses. The image of Christ as high priest is slowly built up by the author over the course of the epistle.

> ...We have a great high priest who has passed through the heavens, Jesus, the Son of God... (Heb 4:14)

With his glorification, Christ becomes the high priest. The divine investiture is the divine oracle of Ps 110:

> So also Christ did not exalt himself to be made a high priest, but was appointed by him who said to him, "You are my Son, today I have begotten you"[14]; as he says in another place, "You are a priest forever, after the order of Melchizedek."[15] (Heb 5:5)

Jesus is the high priest who enters the sanctuary once for all, through offering himself up:

> For it was fitting that we should have such a high priest, holy, blameless, unstained, separated from sinners, exalted above the heavens. He has no need, like those high priests, to offer sacrifices daily, first for his own sins and then for those of the people; he did this once for all when he offered up himself. (Heb 7:26-27)

Jesus is thus different from all the types of priesthood, both pagan and Jewish, that preceded him.

> He entered once for all into the Holy Place, taking not the blood of goats and calves but his own blood, thus securing an eternal redemption. For if the sprinkling of defiled persons with the blood of goats and bulls and with the ashes of a heifer sanctifies for the purification

> of the flesh, how much more shall the blood of Christ,
> who through the eternal Spirit offered himself without
> blemish to God, purify your conscience from dead
> works to serve the living God. (Heb 9: 12-14)

As the high priest, Christ fulfills the Old Testament
sacrificial system by his sacrifice for sin. The author
of Hebrews here also restates the Old Testament principle that "without the shedding of blood there is no
forgiveness of sin."[16]

Thus the hereditary priesthood of the Old Testament
comes to an end, and a new priesthood, directly appointed by God after the order of Melchizedek, begins.
The Old Testament priesthood is fulfilled in the person
of Jesus Christ, who offers himself "once for all." And
thus the bloody sacrifices of the Old Testament also
come to an end, replaced by new, "unbloody, reasonable" offerings, as we hear each time that we celebrate
the eucharistic liturgy: "Also we offer you this spiritual
worship without shedding of blood..." (Anaphora of
St. John Chrysostom).[17]

Having completed his earthly task, Jesus has ascend-
ed to heaven, where, as high priest, he sits at the right
hand of the Father:

> But when Christ had offered for all time a single
> sacrifice for sins, he sat down at the right hand of
> God... For by a single offering he has perfected for all
> time those who are sanctified. (Heb 10:12, 14)

Through his once for all priestly offering, Christ
has brought forgiveness to humanity. This is the reality we are brought into when we are baptized for the
remission of sins,[18] when we are born of water and
the Spirit,[19] when we put on Christ,[20] thus becoming
members of Christ's Body, the Church.[21] The author of

Hebrews describes the new covenant inaugurated by Christ, as prophesied in the Old Testament:

> "This is the covenant that I will make with them after those days, says the Lord: I will put my laws on their hearts, and write them on their minds," then he adds, "I will remember their sins and their misdeeds no more." (Heb 10:16-17, quoting Jer 31:33-34)

Christ, therefore, is presented as the ultimate high priest, both in the sense that he is the perfect model of priesthood and in that he brings the Old Testament sacrificial order to an end by offering himself as the once for all sacrifice. He both fulfills and transforms the priesthood. "For you are the one who offers and is offered," we pray in the liturgy.[22] He inaugurates a new covenant, a new law, which is written in our hearts.[23]

The Priesthood of the Laity

In the Epistle to the Hebrews

Having concluded his long exposition about the priesthood of Christ, the author describes its implications for us:

> Therefore, brethren, since we have confidence to enter the sanctuary by the blood of Jesus, by the new and living way which he opened for us through the curtain,[24] that is, through his flesh, and since we have a great priest over the house of God, let us draw near with a true heart in full assurance of faith, with our hearts sprinkled clean from an evil conscience and our bodies washed with pure water.[25] Let us hold fast the confession of our hope without wavering, for he who promised is faithful; and let us consider how to stir up one another to love and good works, not neglecting to meet together,[26] as is the habit of some, but encouraging one another, and all the more as you

see the Day[27] drawing near. (Heb 10:19-25)

By our own incorporation through baptism into the Body of Christ, the Church, we have not only become members of Christ, but we have a share in the priesthood of Christ.[28] We are, as we learned from I Peter, "a royal priesthood" (1 Pet 2:9; also 2:5). Like Christ, we are now able to "enter the sanctuary" – where only priests could enter before! Now we can actually meet God in a way that no one before Christ was able:

> For you have not come to what may be touched, a blazing fire, and darkness, and gloom, and a tempest, and the sound of a trumpet, and a voice…[29] But you have come to Mount Zion and to the city of the living God, the heavenly Jerusalem, and to innumerable angels in festal gathering, and to the assembly of the firstborn who are enrolled in heaven, and to a judge who is God of all, and to the spirits of just men made perfect, and to Jesus, the mediator of a new covenant, and to the sprinkled blood[30] that speaks more graciously than the blood of Abel. (Heb 12: 18, 22-24)

Christians are called to receive and to accept this news:

> Therefore let us be grateful for receiving a kingdom that cannot be shaken, and thus let us offer to God acceptable worship, with reverence and awe… (Heb 12: 28)

The final chapter of Hebrews is an exhortation to Christian virtue, in which Christians are called to do what Christ did. True Christian worship consists of doing for others.[31] Then, after exhorting the faithful to avoid false teachings, the author, using strongly cultic language, compares the task of Christians with the priestly task of Christ himself:

> We have an altar from which those who serve the

tent[32] have no right to eat. For the bodies of those
animals whose blood is brought into the sanctuary
by the high priest as a sacrifice for sin are burned
outside the camp. So Jesus also suffered outside the
gate in order to sanctify the people through his own
blood. Therefore let us also go forth to him outside
the camp and bear the abuse he endured. For here
we have no lasting city, but we seek the city which
is to come. Through him then let us continually offer
up a sacrifice of praise[33] to God, that is, the fruit of
lips that acknowledge his name. Do not neglect to do
good and to share what you have, for such sacrifices
are pleasing to God. (Heb 13:10-16)

Thus, as Christians who share in Christ's priesthood,
we are called to share in Christ's sacrifice by accepting
the suffering which those who follow Christ have always had to endure. We are called to share in Christ's
sacrifice by praising God. We are called to share in
Christ's sacrifice by doing good deeds. The language
here is totally sacrificial, using terms such as "altar
food," "sacrifice of praise," etc. These terms refer to the
various communion sacrifices of the Old Testament,
which are now seen as fulfilled in the person and ministry of Christ, and in the Christian community, the
Body of Christ. Our priestly task as Christians, therefore, is to carry on Christ's own mission of bringing
God's sacrificial love into the world in which we live, at
home, in the workplace, in society at large.

In Liturgy[34]

Priesthood, as we saw above, belongs first to Christ,
who is the high priest, and secondly to all the baptized
faithful, the royal priesthood. Yet, in the context of the
liturgical life of the Orthodox Church, priesthood is
typically identified with ordained clergy, particularly

bishops and priests, who have the authority to preside over the eucharistic liturgy and other sacraments
and services. For the sake of order, it is necessary for
someone to preside. The function of ordained *orders*
(bishops, presbyters, deacons, etc.) is necessary to pre-
serve *order*. "All things should be done decently and
in order," St. Paul tells the Corinthians.[35] And so, from
earliest times, the Church has had a variety of ministries, and the primary duty of bishops, and eventually
presbyters as well, was to preside over the eucharistic
liturgy. One of the earliest titles for the bishop, in fact,
was "president" (in Greek, *proestamenos*), i.e., "the one
who presides."[36]

Now to preside at the liturgy is not the same as to
exercise a priestly function. If we recall that the primary function of priesthood is to offer sacrifices and to
serve as the intermediary between God and humanity,
then it becomes clear that, in the liturgy, this function
is exercised not by the bishop or presbyter alone, but
by Jesus Christ, the high priest who offered himself up
once for all, or by the entire assembly, which is the corporate Body of Christ. This becomes evident when one
looks at the liturgical texts.

First, liturgical prayer is nearly always in the first person plural, indicating that it is the prayer of the entire
community. Prayers that use the first person singular
are all later additions to the services, typically consisting of pious private devotions. "In peace, let *us* pray
to the Lord," the deacon intones at the beginning. He
then continues with a series of petitions, all addressed
to the entire assembly, asking *them* to pray for different
intentions. Thus, in this most common form of liturgical prayer, the entire community is carrying out its
priestly duty to offer up prayers and intercessions for

the whole world.

The active, priestly role of the entire assembly is even more evident during the anaphora, the great eucharistic prayer. Here, again, the first person plural is used throughout, indicating that this is the prayer of the entire assembly.

> Remembering therefore this our Savior's command and all that has been done for us: the cross, the tomb, the resurrection on the third day, the ascension into heaven, the sitting at the right hand, the second and glorious coming again;
>
> *Offering*[37] you your own of your own – in all things and for all things[38] –
>
> We praise you, we bless you, we give thanks to you, O Lord, and we pray to you, our God.

The chief action, expressed by the active verbs, is done by the entire assembly as they sing the response: "We praise… we bless… we give thanks… we pray." Few people today are even aware that this response is an integral part of the anaphora, and not simply a pious response sung while the clergy continue their recitation of the anaphora. Grammatically, this is all one sentence, with the active verbs sung by the assembly.

It is vital to note here the importance of the gathered assembly, in which clergy and laity act as one. The presiding bishop or presbyter who proclaims these words is doing so in the name of the whole gathering. The "we," which is the grammatical subject of the sentence, includes all who gather, and not just the clergy. This is made all the more evident by the fact that the active verbs are sung by the people, or by the choir in their name. For most of the church's history, these responses would be sung by the entire congregation, and it is only in recent centuries that choirs have taken over this function.

How is it that we praise, bless and give thanks? As the grammatical structure makes clear, we do these things precisely by "remembering" all the things that God has done for us. "Do this in memory of me," Jesus tells his disciples at the Last Supper. Each time that we celebrate the Lord's Supper, the Eucharist, we remember, we call to mind, God's saving activity. And as we remember all these things, we make them present, real, and effective for us today. Remembering, therefore, is an essential task for all Christians, for it is only by always keeping in mind that we are God's creatures and that he has done everything for us, including sending his own Son to die on the cross that we can live. If we forget God, then we are cut off from the source of life and, like a flower separated from its roots, we quickly die.

Precisely because we remember everything that God has done for us, we offer to him that which is already his – "Your own of your own." This act of offering is central, because it is by remembering and offering that we are able to "praise, bless, and thank God." Here again, the gathered assembly, the liturgical "we," is the active agent. The offering is not done by the clergy, but by the entire assembly, led by the bishop or presbyter who recites the prayer *in their name*. The priestly function of offering is exercised by the entire priestly people, the royal priesthood. By celebrating the eucharistic liturgy, by remembering God's saving activity, by making their offering, the people perform their priestly role, which has been given to them at baptism.

Liturgy is the work of the entire people of God (the

laos tou theou), and not, as was the case in Jewish antiquity, the task of a clerical caste. Liturgy, and this is
implied by the Greek word *leitourgia*, literally means
"common work," or "work on behalf of the community." The function of the ordained clergy is to lead the
gathered assembly in performing their priestly function of praising and giving thanks to God, of offering
prayers and intercessions on behalf of all creation. This
is what is implied, as well, in the notion of recapitulation, according to which Jesus Christ is the New Adam,
who brings humanity out of its fallen state and restores
the communion between God and humanity that had
been broken by sin.[39] Through Christ, humanity can
once again share in God's creating activity. Thus humanity, or at least those who hear Christ's message,
receives new birth through baptism. We become members of Christ's body and are now able to resume our
priestly role at the head of God's creation. In baptism,
every Christian comes to share in the priesthood that
belongs to Christ.[40]

The way in which liturgical services are celebrated,
however, often conceals these essential facts. This is
particularly the case with the anaphora at the eucharistic liturgy. In much of the Orthodox world, this
prayer is read silently, interrupted by a few exclama-
tions which serve to indicate that it is time for a sung
response. Often, the anaphora is considered to be a
"private prayer," or read in a language that is incom-
prehensible. Fortunately, thanks primarily to the writings of Fr. Alexander Schmemann,[41] this has begun to
change, and, in an increasing number of Orthodox par-
ishes, both in America and in traditionally Orthodox
lands, all or part of the anaphora is read aloud so that
all can hear. And in America, English is rapidly becom-

ing the standard liturgical language.

The priestly role of the laity has also been marginalized with the expansion of the role of the cantor or choir. During much of the church's history, all the responses were sung by the entire congregation.[42] They sang the "Lord, have mercy" in response to the deacon's petitions. They sang the refrains to the antiphons. They sang the responses to the eucharistic prayer. In the last three or four centuries, choirs (in Slavic practice) and cantors (in Greek practice) have almost completely taken over. As a result, congregations have been reduced to passive spectators, and the sense of the entire community being an active participant in liturgical services has simply been lost. All too often today, liturgical worship is reduced to a show put on by the clergy and the singers. No wonder so many parishioners either remain unmoved by the services, or even alienated! What is needed, therefore, is a rediscovery of the laity's essential, active role in the liturgy.

In the World

The priestly character of the laity, so clearly expressed in Scripture and in the liturgical tradition of the Orthodox Church, needs to be recovered in Christian consciousness. We are called to live out our priesthood in day to day life. In our modern, secularistic world, we tend to segregate our religious life from our everyday life. We practice our faith by going to church for an hour or two each week, but then we shed our religious identity as we step outside the doors of the church. Yet it is precisely in the world, in the family, at the workplace, in the public sphere, that the priestly role of the laity is most central.

Why is this so? We are Christians because, through

our baptism, we have "put on Christ." We have become members of his Body, the Church, and thus, through us, Jesus Christ remains present in the world. Just as Christ was empowered with the Holy Spirit at his baptism in the Jordan, so we too, in our baptism, receive the gift of the Holy Spirit:

> Do you not know that your body is a temple of the Holy Spirit within you, which you have from God? You are not your own; you were bought with a price. So glorify God in your body. (1 Cor 6:19-20)

Every baptized Christian, therefore, is a sign of God's presence in the world. This is affirmed by Scripture, realized in the liturgy, and it must be lived out in the world. Every Christian is a priest, called to bring God's divine love and forgiveness to a world which lives in sin and darkness. Every Christian is called to this priestly, mediatory task.

As the author of Hebrews points out, we are called to share in Christ's sacrifice. This inevitably includes suffering, because just as Jesus was rejected and abused, so the Christian will be rejected and abused. This is as true today as it was in the age of persecution. We are called to offer our sacrifice of praise to God as Christ praised his Father at every moment in his life, and we must do this not only in church, but in every moment of our lives. We are called to do good by laying down our life for the neighbor, as Christ laid down his life for us. We should visit the sick, feed the hungry, clothe the naked, help the poor, and reflect God's love wherever we happen to be. These functions are *priestly* functions which we acquire through our baptism into Christ.

All too often, we absolve ourselves of these responsibilities by saying that these are tasks that properly belong to ordained clergy. After all, that is what we pay them to do. And, indeed, ordained clergy do have to do all these things. But they must do them not because they are ordained, but because they are themselves baptized Christians, members of the priestly, royal people of God.

The chief function of the ordained is to maintain and promote order within the church. They teach, they preach, they preside at parish or diocesan events, they are responsible for maintaining discipline. All these dimensions are necessary for the well-being of the church, but there is more. Their task, the task of the church as a whole, is to carry out the task for which Christ came into the world – to reconcile God and humanity, to offer up God's self-emptying love for the life of the world. Ultimately, therefore, the task of the clergy is nothing less than to enable all the baptized to exercise this priestly ministry of Christ, which each of us receives in the baptismal font. Ordained clergy carry out their mission within the local church community. We, baptized Christians, are called to exercise our priestly vocation out in the world.

Thus, one need not be ordained in order to live out one's priestly vocation. Whatever we choose to do – whether as a laborer, an engineer, a doctor, a lawyer, or a teacher – we are called to act as Christ acted. Wherever we are – whether at home, at the workplace, in the park – we are called to reflect the presence and the love of Christ.

Notes

1 From the Greek word *laos,* meaning "people."
2 The notion of Christ as "high priest" is developed in the Epistle

to the Hebrews – cf. Heb 2:17; 3:1; 4:14; 5:1-10; 6:20; 7:26-28; 8:1-3; 9:11-22; 10:21. In the rest of the New Testament, this notion is only implicit, and Christ is depicted as the "Suffering Servant" based on Isa 53, or in his (priestly) role as fulfilling the sacrifice for sin, based on Exod 24:8. It is highly significant that these latter themes are particularly evident in the descriptions of the Last Supper – cf. Joachim Jeremias, *The Eucharistic Words of Jesus* (Philadelphia: Fortress Press, 1977). For a broader discussion of this theme, see Jerome Kodell, *The Eucharist in the New Testament* (Wilmington, DE: Michael Glazier, 1988).

3 On the biblical understanding of priesthood, see Raymond E. Brown, *Priest and Bishop: Biblical Reflections* (New York: Paulist Press, 1970). On the evolution of the understanding of the term "laity," see Alexandre Faivre, *The Emergence of the Laity in the Early Church* (Mahwah, NJ: Paulist Press, 1990).

4 See Gal 3:27.

5 For Orthodox Christians, worship of God constitutes the central activity of the church. Through the liturgical act of baptism, we become members of the Body of Christ, the Church. Through our participation in the eucharistic life of the church, we affirm and realize our membership in this body. Thus, our true identity is revealed and fulfilled. See, for example, Alexander Schmemann, *For the Life of the World: Sacraments and Orthodoxy* (Crestwood, NY: St. Vladimir's Seminary Press, 1973). For a more general discussion of this approach, see John D. Zizioulas, *Being as Communion* (Crestwood, NY: St. Vladimir's Seminary Press, 1985).

6 For a general discussion on priesthood in the Old Testament, see Raymond E. Brown, *Priest and Bishop: Biblical Reflections* (New York: Paulist Press, 1970), 5-13.

7 See Gen 22:2; 31:54.

8 Gen 14:18.

9 Ps 110:4.

10 Heb 5:6; 5:10; 6:20; 7:1; 7:10; 7:11; 7:15; 7:17; 7:21.

11 Deut 33:8-10.

12 1 Sam 14:41-42. This function of the priesthood disappeared after the construction of the Second Temple following the Babylonian exile.

13 Though not focusing on the priesthood as such, the Gospel of John, particularly in ch. 6, has as its central theme that Christ is the

sole mediator between God and humanity.

14 Ps 2:7.

15 Ps 110:4. Melchizedek was a Canaanite priest-king who blessed Abram and greeted him with an offering of bread and wine (see Gen 14:17-20). This mysterious figure was subsequently interpreted as a messianic prophecy in Ps 110 and Heb 7:1-17. The point here is that Melchizedek does not belong to the hereditary, Levitical priesthood, which has now been superseded.

16 Heb 9:22.

17 English text taken from *The Divine Liturgy of Our Father among the Saints John Chrysostom* (Oxford: Oxford University Press, 1995), 33.

18 "I acknowledge one baptism for the remission of sins," Nicene Creed.

19 "Unless one is born of water and the Spirit, he cannot enter the kingdom of God" (John 3:5).

20 "For as many of you as were baptized into Christ have put on Christ" (Gal 3:27).

21 See 1 Cor 12:12ff.

22 Prayer of the Cherubic Hymn, *Liturgy of Our Father among the Saints John Chrysostom*, op. cit., 23.

23 See Rom 2:15 and 2 Cor 3:2-3.

24 The reference here is to the veil in the Temple which hid the Holy of Holies, where God's holiness dwelt.

25 An obvious reference to our baptism!

26 This refers to the regular assemblies of Christians for the celebration of the Lord's Supper, the Eucharist.

27 The Second Coming of Christ. Early Christians lived with the expectation that Christ's return was imminent. With the development of the annual feast of Easter (Pascha) in the second century, Christians came to associate this day in particular with the expected parousia. In contemporary Orthodox practice, this sense remains strong, as we can see in the oft-repeated hymn, "Behold, the Bridegroom comes at midnight..." (Troparion for the Bridegroom Matins of Holy Week).

28 "For as many of you as were baptized into Christ have put on Christ," Gal 3:27.

29 These refer to the various ways in which God revealed himself and spoke in the Old Testament.

30 A reference to the blood shed by Christ, as well as to the eucharistic gathering, in which Christians remember and celebrate this new covenant.

31 Heb 13:1-6; see also Heb 10:19-25).

32 Some sources read "tabernacle." This refers to the Jews, whose worship is in the Temple.

33 A term referring to the eucharistic liturgy – see the introductory dialogues to the anaphoras of both John Chrysostom and Basil the Great.

34 I use the term "liturgy" in its broad sense, as referring not only to the eucharistic liturgy, but to the whole liturgical life of the church, including the daily, weekly, and festal cycles of worship. It is in the eucharistic liturgy, however, that the priesthood of the laity is most clearly expressed. For an excellent overview of the Byzantine eucharistic liturgy, see Alexander Schmemann, *The Eucharist: Sacrament of the Kingdom* (Crestwood, NY: St. Vladimir's Seminary Press, 1988).

35 1 Cor 14:40.

36 Cf. John D. Zizioulas, *Being as Communion* (Crestwood, NY: St. Vladimir's Seminary Press, 1985), esp. ch. 4: "Eucharist and Catholicity," 143-169.

37 The contemporary Greek text, as well as most English translations, render "offering" in the indicative "we offer." See, for example, the official text most commonly used in the Orthodox Church in America (*The Divine Liturgy According to St. John Chrysostom* [Russian Orthodox Greek Catholic Church of America, 1967], 59); in the Antiochian Orthodox Christian Archdiocese (*The Liturgikon* [Englewood, NJ: Antiochian Orthodox Christian Archdiocese, 1989], 287); the Romanian Episcopate (*The Divine Liturgy According to Saint John Chrysostom* [Jackson, MI: The Romanian Orthodox Episcopate of America, 1975, rep. 1987, 1990], 83; and the Holy Cross faculty edition commonly used in the Greek Orthodox Archdiocese (*The Divine Liturgy* [Brookline, MA, Holy Cross Orthodox Press, 1985], 24. The original Greek text, as well as the Slavonic to the present day, use the participial form: *prospherontes*, Slavonic: *prinosiashche*. Among recent English translations, only the Oxford edition cited in this essay, as well as the recent SCOBA translation (unpublished) use the original, participial form.

38 In Greek, *kata panta kai dia panta*. The meaning of this phrase

is not clear, and it could also mean "always and everywhere." Grammatically, the phrase modifies the active verbs, "we praise, we bless..."

39 See particularly St. Paul's Epistle to the Romans, chs. 5-6. This notion is further developed in the second century by St. Irenaeus of Lyons in Book V of his *Against Heresies*.

40 See A. Schmemann, *Of Water and the Spirit: A Liturgical Study of Baptism* (Crestwood, NY: St. Vladimir's Seminary Press, 1974), 94-99.

41 See particularly his posthumously published book, *The Eucharist: Sacrament of the Kingdom* (Crestwood, NY: St. Vladimir's Seminary Press, 1988). Fr. Alexander is also the father of the modern eucharistic revival within Orthodoxy, which has made possible much greater and more frequent reception of communion.

42 On popular participation in the liturgy, see John F. Baldovin's study, *The Urban Character of Christian Worship: The Origin, Development, and Meaning of Stational Liturgy* (=Orientalia Christiana Analecta 228) (Rome: Pontificium Institutum Studiorum Orientalium, 1987).

Contributors

Khaled Anatolios is Associate Professor of Historical Theology at Weston Jesuit School of Theology, Cambridge, MA. He is the author of *Athanasius: The Coherence of his Thought* (Routledge, 1998 & 2005) and the *Athanasius* volume of the "Early Church Fathers" series (Routledge, 2004).

John Barnet is Associate Professor of New Testament, St. Vladimir's Orthodox Theological Seminary, Crestwood, NY. He is the author of *Not the Righteous but Sinners: M. M. Bakhtin's Theory of Aesthetics and the Problem of Reader-Character Interaction in Matthew's Gospel*, published by T & T Clark International.

Deborah Malacky Belonick is the author of *Feminism in Christianity: An Orthodox Christian Perspective* and has contributed to several books and theological journals. A well-known retreat leader, she currently is the Associate Editor at St. Vladimir's Seminary Press.

Ann Mitsakos Bezzerides is Director of the Office of Vocation and Ministry at Hellenic College, Brookline, MA. She has been a lecturer in Religious Education at St. Vladimir's Orthodox Theological Seminary, Crestwood, NY, and is a Ph.D. candidate in Theology and Education at Boston College, Chestnut Hill, MA.

Fr. Stanley Samuel Harakas is Archbishop Iakovos Professor of Orthodox Theology, *Emeritus* at Holy Cross Greek Orthodox School of Theology, Brookline, MA, having taught Orthodox Christian Ethics there for thirty years prior to his retirement. He is the author of several foundational books in the field of Orthodox Christian ethics, including *Toward Transfigured Life* and *Living the Faith.*

Demetrios S. Katos is Assistant Professor of Religious Studies at Hellenic College, Brookline, MA, where he teaches courses in Orthodox theology. His research interests lie in the history and theology of early Christianity.

Paul Meyendorff is Associate Dean for Academic Affairs and the Alexander Schmemann Professor of Liturgical Theology at St. Vladimir's Orthodox Theological Seminary, Crestwood, NY. He is the author of several books and many articles, and travels widely to lecture on Orthodox liturgy.

Fr. Theodore Stylianopoulos is Archbishop Iakovos Professor of Orthodox Theology and Professor of New Testament at Holy Cross Greek Orthodox School of Theology, Brookline, MA. He has taught New Testament and other courses at Holy Cross and Hellenic College since 1967. His latest book is *The Way of Christ* (Holy Cross Orthodox Press, 2002).

Fr. Paul Nadim Tarazi is Professor of Old Testament at St. Vladimir's Orthodox Theological Seminary, Crestwood, NY. He is the author of introductory series on the Old and New Testaments, and commentaries on Galatians and I Thessalonians (St. Vladimir's Seminary Press).